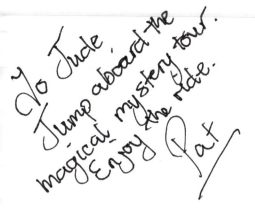

C/o Jude,
Jump aboard the
magical mystery tour.
Enjoy the ride.
Pat

D0302619

DANCE ON TOES
IN THE FROSTED GRASS

extracts from a memory journal

PATRICIA E SMITH

PUBLISHED BY ERIDRON PUBLISHING

First published by Eridron Publishing 2013
ISBN 978-0-9926406-0-62013

Copyright © Patricia E. Smith 2013
www.patriciaesmith.com

Printed and distributed by www.authorsonline.co.uk
This book is also available in e-book format and kindle,
details of which are also available at www.authorsonline.co.uk

about the author

Patricia E. Smith is an author, a practitioner of energy work and also an amateur artist. She lives near the university town of St Andrews in Scotland. Through her work as a facilitator of inspirational workshops she encourages people to come together to learn, share knowledge and experience working with higher dimensional energies in a safe and secure environment. Her factual writing is seen by others as revelatory and motivational whilst her fictional work is enjoyed by many. Writing has been and will continue to be the major driving force in her daily life.

Her novel The Star Seed Legacy was published in 2006. It is the first of what will eventually become a fantasy fiction trilogy. Her second book Dance on Toes in the Frosted Grass is taken from extracts of a memory journal. It relates in detail to some of the more memorable experiences of the spiritual journey Patricia first began over twenty years ago.

The extracts she includes in her book are diverse in content and fascinating for anyone who may be considering undertaking just such a journey for themselves. Each individual extract conveys different aspects of Patricias path. It records her rapid expansion of consciousness and subsequent spiritual growth. Offering intriguing insights the book takes the reader on a magical mystery tour of self discovery to reveal the truth within.

Through her daily work with different energies Patricia hopes to encourage others to take the first step on the path to their own truth. By simply choosing to explore the avenues which open up in life people can discover for themselves how extraordinary life is. Without anything to limit them anyone can transcend rigid belief patterning and become the beautiful beings of light they were always meant to be.

www.patriciaesmith.com

acknowledgments

My own extraordinary journey would never have started without the love shared between Anne MacDonald Denver and John Christopher Denver. They were instrumental in encouraging me to value the life I had been given and to always be sensitive and understanding towards those less fortunate than myself. I want to thank them for the wisdom they imparted and for their generosity of spirit in gifting me their love.

This book is dedicated to them and to my grandmother, Mary Martin Maxwell Todd/ Shield.

To my dear and much loved friend Sheila. I am eternally grateful for your friendship and generous, giving heart. What a wondrous and crazy journey it has been.

To the special group of people who were guided to accompany and assist me on my road to spiritual awareness and fulfilment. Thank you for sharing your experiences and life affirming knowledge.

To the energy workers who quietly go about speaking their Truth and spreading the Light.

To my beautiful daughters so they might experience why I chose to lay down my footprints and walk the spiritual path. You fill my heart with such joy and inspire me in so many ways.

To Joshua in the knowledge that the many special gifts he possesses will help promote change and bring a sense of unity to our universe once more.

To Stewart for his proofreading / editorial skills.

To Chris for coming up with such imaginative designs.

Finally to Shoshana, Carol and Isobel in the hope that the road they now travel is as blessed and beautiful as they always knew it would be.

contents

Extract no. 1:
In the beginning

I love to write. I have always loved it. The thrill of hands hovering over the lined, virgin pad fills me with a real sense of excitement and anticipation. Initially, I write in long hand. It satisfies the surge and transitory rush of creativity. That sensation, as the stomach does somersaults and back flips in recognition of those first tentative forays, is a joyful thing. The moment the seed of an idea stares back from those very same lines is unlike any other feeling. For me, writing never palls. Over the years it has been the one constant in my life. It is one of the few things which will really nurture me both on creative and other levels. It requires discipline, but it is a good sort of discipline. It inspires me to get up and get on with the day. There is nothing quite like the unpredictability and promise of unfolding drama of the written word to get the creative juices flowing.

Encouraging and motivating the old grey cells to extricate the first few words for any new piece of written work is sometimes difficult. Unless one is entirely reconciled and comfortable with the content, it is very easy to come seriously unstuck before one even starts. Every successful story invites its audience to go on a journey of discovery with the author. Everything hinges on a compelling storyline, skilful usage of language and the correct word selection. Seldom will the words voluntarily rush forward of their own volition without some gentle persuasion and encouragement. Coaxing is required by the bucket load. Even after the words have struggled so valiantly to come to the surface and finally reveal themselves, all too often those meritorious little gems can end up being at the mercy of the stroke of a pen, or removed from the screen by the simple act of hitting the delete button. To face such ignominy after such effort does seem unjust.

In order to move the story I wish to tell forward I will first of all have to go back in time. This story will not take the traditional fictional route. Instead, I will take you on what for me will be a personal journey through some of the written extracts from my own memory journal. I will share with you some of the more memorable experiences I have had along the way. This will help explain how my connections with angelic beings, ascended masters, planetary beings, star family, elementals, nature energies, and the recent return of unicorn energy, helped to expand my consciousness and understanding of such things. It will also reveal how my heart opened up to embrace life in a way it had never done so before.

Before I get completely ahead of myself by launching straight into the narrative, and also to bring some sense of sequential order to events, let me touch fleetingly upon the early years of my life.

the moment it all began

As men and women eventually returned from the hideousness of war, and attempted to gain some normality in their lives once more, history might be inclined to say there was a defining inevitability about what happened next. There was a massive population explosion. It was my destiny to be a part of that very same explosion. The moment I was born I was labeled. I became what was most commonly referred to as a post-war boomer child.

moving on

I was relatively shy growing up and, though I had an older brother, because of the seven-year age gap between us, I often felt like an only child. In common with other children my own age, there were many events in my young life that would leave me feeling less certain or lacking in confidence. My father worked away from home a great deal and my mother held down a full time job. As a result, my maternal grandmother played a large part in my upbringing. It was to her I would invariably turn. Memories of her have not faded with time. I can still remember the softness of her small, crippled hands and the sweet scent of lavender from the delicately embroidered hankies she always had at the ready. When it came to wiping the tears or plastering a bloodied knee, she was always there. Any sense of confusion or hurt I might be feeling was instantly allayed. My grandmother definitely had the knack of soothing the injured soul. Words that comforted were seldom far away.

Looking back on events, I think subconsciously I probably recognised my grandmother had a lot of suppressed emotions. She found it difficult to express her feelings, or let anyone see behind the protective wall she had erected around herself. Although she was not a 'hugging feeling' type of person, my relationship with my grandmother was always a special one. Everyone in the family recognised that. As I reflect on our relationship, a little flag pops up to remind me of something. Even now, from my adult perspective, trying to be exact about the way our relationship was is not easy to put into words. It probably should be, but it is not.

I suppose I had always had a sense of my grandmother and me connecting at a level that precluded the participation of other members of our family. It surprises me that on one level I was consciously aware of this exclusion existing, yet on some other level had no understanding as to why this exclusion existed. I have little or no recollection at all of how this affected others in the family. Did they feel excluded? Were they even aware of it? I simply do not know.

What strikes me as really strange, and a little sad, is the fact that until I entered my double-digit years I have no memory at all of anything other than a cursory interaction between my brother and my grandmother. We all lived under the same roof so there obviously had to be connection between them. I just cannot recall what their relationship with each other was like.

It was around the time of my tenth or eleventh birthday when several pieces of the jigsaw of my life began to suddenly fall into place. I became the recipient of certain information about my grandmother. Revelations indicated she was the possessor of something quite special; she was psychic. Do not ask me how I made this important discovery. The great event was not heralded by trumpets blowing and banners flying. I am pretty certain that my grandmother did not inform me of the fact. Somehow, my discovery just happened along. There I was, minding my own business having absolutely no knowledge of 'psychic', when suddenly the information was there inside my head. Of course, just because I had this information it did not mean I understood it. I had no real idea how being psychic worked or what it meant. Was it something everyone in the family had or was it only given to one member of the family? Did the grandmothers of my school friends all have this psychic 'thing' or was it just mine? More importantly, was this psychic 'thing' something that I would get one day? I didn't even know if my mother and father were aware my grandmother was psychic. Perhaps it was all a huge secret my grandmother wanted to keep hidden and to herself. I wondered if she had picked up on the fact that her secret was out. Initially, I felt a little awkward, knowing something about her I probably shouldn't. For a while I could not look her straight in the eye. Should I say something to her and let her know I knew, or would she think I was just being silly? Being the child I was, I had no real idea if me knowing about her secret really mattered anyway? In the end, I said nothing.

Once I discovered what I did about my grandmother, I appropriated her secret and turned it into our secret. I don't think I spent any time or effort exploring what psychic might have meant. Even though I sensed the meaning of it was probably important, it had no meaning for me. On the few occasions I did give it thought I was no further forward in my understanding. Was psychic a word or a feeling, or just something my imagination had dreamt up? I had not a clue. Although I was probably ill prepared to receive such information, I sensed I must have been given that information for a reason. At the time, I did not know why. Eventually, all that changed. Although it was not an immediate thing, over the coming years the word psychic began to integrate itself at a conscious level.

Other changes began to take place in my young life. Certain abilities of my very own chose that time to gradually reveal themselves. I knew something was happening and changing inside me. Whatever that something was helped certain questions to line up and position themselves. I really wanted to know whether my friends were making similar discoveries about themselves, or was I alone? Were they experiencing things just as I was? Could they be having the same sort of feelings as me? Was this all part of growing up? Even if it was, would I ever be able to pluck up enough courage to ask them? Probably the fear of being ridiculed became the determining factor, and in the end I kept what I was experiencing to myself.

Without being told, I realised something else was afoot. It was all to do with my grandmother. I did not need to be coerced in any way into accepting that somehow she and I shared something no one else did. It was more a feeling than anything else that we knew 'things' others were not privy to. There was no other way of putting it. This was as close as I would ever get to expressing in words exactly what I was experiencing. It was during this time my grandmother died. With the best intentions in the world, my mother bundled me off to stay with family friends while the funeral took place. It really affected me. It was my time to feel excluded and apart from my family. I grieved the exclusion and the fact I was unable to say farewell to my grandmother. To my young mind nothing would ever be the same again. When I returned home the emptiness in the house matched the emptiness I was feeling inside my young heart. My mother was standing at the door waiting for me. Though she raised a smile for me, I could tell she was sad. We held onto each other and cried for the longest time. I can still remember the warmth and soft familiarity of her body and the delicate smell of the perfume she always wore.

With the death of my grandmother things did change in my life. Although the security and certainty of her always being there in the physical had gone, I could still visit my memories. An important and precious part of my life was over. It was time to move on.

Approaching my mid teens I began to feel a little more comfortable and relaxed with the whole growing up process. I started to gain some confidence and feel a lot more positive about myself. The awkwardness and gaucheness so often associated with those early teenage years were gradually left behind. There were other benefits to reaching that age. For the first time in my life I began to really believe in myself as a person in my own right. It did not stop at that. Something else was going on, something which really excited me and opened my mind up to all sorts of possibilities. I am not quite sure how it happened, or exactly where it had come from, but suddenly I became aware of important new inner knowledge. I knew without a shadow of doubt that my life could and would change if I wanted it to. Some untold thing or event would one day just happen and somehow change my life, and the living of that life, forever.

Realisation and acceptance of that knowing found its way into information for the future segment of my brain. I try to remember if any of this actually activated an immediate change to the way I looked at life and determine that in all probability it did not. The fact was, whatever happened in the future bore little relevance to living in the present. It was enough for me to know that I was in possession of the information. The time for revelation would come around soon enough. For the time being, I took my eyes off the distant horizon of young adulthood and reverted to the enjoyment of being the teenager I was.

What I do remember most about those distant times with any real degree of clarity was the sense of self-belief I had. I had no idea why or how it had decided to attach itself to me, or what had instigated such a belief in my own identity and destiny. Had my upbringing and the influences in my life up to that point been responsible, or were other elements I had yet to consider working quietly behind the scenes? My brother had always had a confident disposition, so had I inherited some similar genetic attribute? One thing I was certain of was the way I felt inside about myself. When the timing was right, I knew I would step out of the shadow of others and find my own place in the world.

Initially, that belief was never stronger than when I was on the cusp of leaving my youth behind and entering adulthood. I had managed to convince myself that I was protected by a voluminous cloak of invincibility. The way I chose to perceive things contributed enormously in me believing the world was definitely my oyster. There was not a mountain in existence that would prove too high to climb, or any obstacle too large for me to dismantle. I could and would conquer everything in the firm knowledge it would bring me closer to my desired destiny. The inner resolve I had to take on the world at anything of my choosing and come out victorious was powerful and deeply entrenched.

So, my first steps into adulthood began. My advancement through the bravado and arrogance of youth were rapidly replaced with the reality of living in the world as a fully paid up adult.

It did not take long for me to realise the path that had promised so much, and on which I had set out with such hope and fervour, was not as straight as I had envisaged. Dreams and aspirations I had about my life automatically becoming a rip-roaring, runaway success remained in part unfulfilled. Don't get me wrong, my adult life had turned out relatively well. In the grand scheme of things, however, if I was to be entirely honest with myself, it just was not as great or meaningful as I thought it would be. Some vital element was missing. I had shared in the success of a happy family life. I had also experienced great joy in my life. Things though, seldom – if ever – stay the same.

As time moved on, events in my life took over and presented me with an entirely new scenario to the one I had anticipated. Dramatic, life-altering events became the reality of the day. I found myself marching to a different drum beat. Every day, it seemed I became more and more conscious of subtle, and not so subtle, shifts taking place within me. Something important was trying to grab hold of my attention. I was not imagining the feeling. It was as though some restless spirit had seen a vacancy sign and started inhabiting the inner workings of my mind and body. I didn't feel any part of me actually belonged to me anymore.

Many people I have spoken to over the years tell me when they reached a certain time in their lives they found themselves facing up to a future where something resembling a nothingness stared right back at them. I know exactly how they felt. That particular abyss and I were very well acquainted. How many times had I visited that place before accepting my life as I knew it no longer gave me what I needed? I knew there had to be something else out there for me which would help to heal the remorseless expansive pit of darkness and feeling of emptiness inside me. Then I remembered something. Was it finally time for the knowingness from my youth to make its appearance and turn my life around? Without any real idea of what lay ahead, I packed up my bags of life memories and walked, albeit hesitantly, into my fourth decade.

I had known for the longest time that some subtle 'things' were infiltrating my thoughts. They could best be described as expansions of some other latent consciousness taking over. I just had no true understanding as to what those particular consciousness 'things' were. They would toy with me, inviting me to play or interact. Just when I thought the 'things' and I might connect and strike up a meaningful dialogue, I found myself being picked up and put to one side again. There was no getting away from the fact that the 'things' were proving pretty elusive. They were masters of the tease. Occasionally, they would offer vague insights into some hidden parts of me. Thoughts would surface and get within reaching distance. All too often that would become a matter of increasing frustration and irritation when, just as quickly as those little nuggets had materialised, so, in a flash, they would dematerialise.

My approach to life had always been fairly pragmatic. How often had my mother told me that "what would be would be" and "what was for me wouldn't go past me". With only a few rare exceptions that pretty much was the way it had panned out. Whilst I had not always followed the lines I had laid down for myself, I had not exactly been over exertive and pushed the boundaries either. After years of seemingly endless wandering and wondering, my life was set on a course to discover a purpose once more. I was determined to be less passive and laid back, and become more absorbed and involved in living and walking along a path I had consciously chosen for myself. The rather misguided presumption that others could or would somehow govern or make decisions for me and the way I would live my life were once and for all laid to rest. From that moment forward, whoever walked alongside me would be invited to. I would walk in my own shoes and create my own footprints.

Finally, I made the conscious connection of having allowed twenty years of my life to pass me by. I could hardly believe that was the length of time it had taken me to fully realise some profound and latent spiritual thing wakening within me. As soon as that connection was made it took no time at all to recognise that the wakening was in reality a reawakening.

thoughts on the weekend ahead

On reflection, I do not believe the timing of the weekend could have been any more perfect. I was not sure if Reiki would prove to be the catalyst for the mysteries of consciousness I sought, but I was well and truly ready to find out.

The thought of the weekend filled me with excitement and a mild sense of nervous anticipation in equal measure. Although I did not know it at the time, those two days spent amongst a group of complete strangers would prove to be both a milestone and turning point in my life. The days would act as a trigger. They would be responsible for revealing the, up until then hidden, aspects of myself and bring about long awaited changes to my life, and how I chose to live that life. The weekend would also set me on the path of exploring and rediscovering myself. From that moment on I would find myself taking on the mantle of being actively and consciously engaged in the living of my life. Although this would be the time I found my life spinning on a sixpence, I was more than ready.

I had an innate sense that I would not have long to wait before remembrances and memories of distant times began to slowly emerge. Through the long narrow tributaries of the brain's complicated mapping system, the journey to find a way back to the forefront of my consciousness would begin. Those very same remembrances and memories had successfully submerged themselves in a state of self-imposed isolation for so long. Over one weekend, the spark of recognition would be re-ignited. Thoughts would reawaken from their slumber and start to put out feelers. Once the trickle of information and knowledge started to filter through, it would not take long for that steady trickle to gain momentum. Trying to control that would not be easy. As I visualised the trickle becoming a raging torrent in full flood, I intuitively knew that no control would be needed. The stampede towards a more conscious way of life and living was about to begin, and I was more than happy to run with that.

the weekend

I remember the glorious autumn morning just as clearly as if it were yesterday. Within a minute or two of leaving the main road behind, my friend and I found ourselves driving along a narrow, but deeply rutted track, heading for the cottage about a mile into Forestry Commission land. As we bumped and scraped our way along the track, the car's suspension was doing its level best to avoid any permanent scarring or damage. As my friend concentrated on getting us both to our destination safely, I had the luxury of being able to lean back, relax and take in the familiar landscape. In my head I sensed the start of waxing lyrical coming on, so I indulged myself.

Overhead, the sky was clear, apart from a few straggly whispers of sporadic trailing cloud. A blanket of delicate dew drops rested softly upon the carpets of burnished copper leaves and dense foliage. Without a word being spoken we slowed down and let the car come to a temporary standstill. For several minutes we just sat there with the engine quietly ticking over, taking in our incredible surroundings. Scotland is a country blessed and bursting at the seams with just such sights, but there was something truly special about this particular one. Everywhere the eye came to rest another beautiful image presented itself. The colours were breathtaking and the sounds of the birds as they chatted and trilled their melodies enchanting. Sometimes there are moments in life when nature surpasses word or description. That day was just such a day. Even the deep, earthy smell of forest floor rising up to seep through the wound-down windows managed to set the senses alight.

My friend and I had set out early for our first Reiki weekend, where we hoped to be attuned to this incredible new, or so we thought at the time, energy we had heard so many people talking about. If ever there was a new buzzword on the lips of those who knew, then Reiki was that word. With little more than a desire to discover more about the offerings of the universe, we started out on our spiritual quest. We might have had a certain naivety about what we were about to undertake, but we were both still savvy enough to know that when it came to alternative energy 'things' we would have to trust our own judgment. We accepted that in some cases all was not always what it appeared to be. Without wishing to denigrate or cause offence, as far as we were aware Reiki was not some wacky, new age hippy thing. It was something entirely different and came with its own unique provenance. It felt right to be going on this course. People we knew to be eminently sensible and intelligent were taking it up. We rationalised that if other sections of society regarded us as all being part of some loony fringe then we would be in some pretty good company.

Reiki was surrounded by an air of mysticism and promise of adventure in untold realms. Whilst these other realms had been a distinct possibility, in my mind's imaginings there still existed a small degree of scepticism. Because I lacked both the knowledge and experience, I suppose what I really wanted was proof of some sort. I did not have an understanding of outright acceptance. What I needed to know, in terms I could readily understand, was what exactly constituted realms and how could they best be defined? Where were they exactly? Did other forms of energies live in these realms, and if they did what were these energies like? In my limited framework of reference these were the questions without answers I wished could be answered. I knew I would not have too long to wait before my thirst for the truth was satiated, even if only in part. I had heard so much about the energy, and a few months previously had had a treatment from a qualified Reiki practitioner. That experience had excited and intrigued me. Now, I wanted to find out for myself if this mystical and magical energy was for me or not. Would my search for the elusive mystery ingredient of life be found? Would Reiki prove to be the great panacea for my expectations?

As it happened, the weekend proved to be something very special. It lived up to, and exceeded, my expectations. Initially, I was not entirely sure what it was I could or should be expecting. Would events have turned out differently had I just gone with a completely open mind and had no expectations in mind? All I definitely did know was that I was ready for the journey. Every part of me just wanted to set the wheels in motion and get things started.

The group that had assembled for the weekend was made up of a fairly mixed bunch. Introductions were made. People did their own instant one-stop assessment of others. Some held back, uncertain or unsure of what was about to take place. It was interesting to watch the silent majority quietly weighing up the slightly more vociferous minority. Everyone eventually began to settle, secure in their own belief that they would soon discover 'things' which would bring about spiritual change and transformation in their lives. Although I instinctively knew that my life would never be the same again after the experiences of the weekend, I was probably more cautiously optimistic than nervous or fearful.

Slender tendrils of anticipation gently wrapped themselves around us. Proceedings were just about to get under way when a pretty young girl entered the room and sat down beside everyone. The host for the day made hasty introductions. The young girl turned out to be her youngest daughter. She smiled at everyone, completely unfazed or perturbed at the sight of such a large group of strangers in her home. Every eye in the group veered towards her. We were all surprised when we learnt her age and also by the fact that she would be joining us. At around ten years old she would be the youngest of the group. No one knew quite how to react to the idea of one so young being included and actually participating in the weekend. I do not suppose for one moment the inclusion of a child was something any of us had given any consideration to. I am sure I was not the only one to feel slightly foolish with the dawning realisation that Reiki wasn't just for the grown ups. Here was an energy which embraced and actively encouraged our acceptance of the participation of children.

Discordant mutterings and mumblings from certain minority quarters had the intended effect. One would have to have been blind, deaf and dumb not to notice. Everyone must have sensed the subtle shift in the whole dynamics and energy of the room. It was difficult to believe that the negative reaction of a couple of people could have impacted so swiftly. They had given little or no thought as to how this might affect our group. It wasn't exactly the start to the day I had envisaged. I must admit I was both surprised and a little disappointed at the turn of events. Were these people really seriously questioning the right of the girl to be there, or was it simply a knee-jerk reaction? It did make me think, though. How could some of those I was about to share a spiritual weekend with be so lacking in grace and vision and so narrow in their thinking? I could only imagine they felt threatened in some way. Perhaps their own personal insecurities led them to doubts over how a child might directly affect the outcome of what they perceived would be 'their' two days. It was either that, or for some reason unknown to the rest of us, they simply did not want her there. I hoped the mutterings would turn out to be a transitory hiccough and not precursors to any form of ill conceived enmity directed towards her. As far as I understood it, the weekend was about coming together to share an experience and in the process discover things about ourselves and our humanity to others. We were there to learn about giving and opening our hearts even further.

I thought the girl enchanting. Whether she realised it or not, her presence definitely had the effect of drawing people into her energy field. Young as she was, it soon became apparent to most of us that there was something quite special about her. It was hard to define exactly what it was that made her stand out. There was no doubting that several of the adults were intrigued by the air of gentle naive serenity she exuded. Some quite possibly might have liked a little bit of that serenity for themselves. The fact she appeared to be so very much wiser than her tender years only helped to further enhance the mystery surrounding her. I was glad to see when we stopped for lunch or tea breaks how easily she slipped out of serene mode and reverted to being the child she was. No one could deny the gentle way she went about things or her contribution to the success of the two days. The lasting impression she would leave me with was one of joy at the way she had reached out and touched my heart.

The biggest surprise came when Charles, the Reiki master, walked in. Before a single word had been spoken I was already facing my second lesson of the day. In my mind I had somehow conjured up this naive, archetypal image of a master who was old and wise and all knowing. He had experienced life and had the wisdom of the world at his fingertips. Was I ever in for a shock! I had not expected a master to look like a lanky, pubescent teenager, nor did I expect to recognise that teenager. I did a quick double-take as my mind registered the confusion it was feeling. I knew this Charles. I looked at him again, taking in his long, dark hair, his assured confident manner and the calm air of certainty he was projecting. Less than a week ago, Charles had been a guest in my home. He had come along with Catherine, a close friend of my eldest daughter. They were boyfriend and girlfriend and utterly besotted with one another, and epitomised the perfect image of love's young dream. Very quickly, I surmised that since Catherine had returned to Paris and her boyfriend had returned to the States two days previously, I knew it was not possible for him to be standing in front of me. Much to my surprise, it appeared that Charles had a double out there he had no knowledge of. It was spooky and a little unnerving. If only geography, circumstance and the powers of the universe had allowed, Charles could have been not only a twin, but an identical twin. Even stranger still was the revelation that both the boyfriend and Charles also shared the same first name.

My recollections of the remainder of the weekend are hazy at best. As I continue writing this down I find it interesting and curious what I do choose to remember. Immediately, my mind latches onto one aspect of the weekend I will not forget in a hurry. The memory of the part played by the dreaded chair will be forever indelibly imprinted on my brain. I ask myself the age old question, knowing and understanding in advance that the response seldom, if ever, varies, why are we so often very much wiser after the event?

On reflection, perhaps I should have tested the suitability and comfort factor of the chair before I made the decision to sit down, but I don't think the thought even entered my head. I just grabbed the first chair closest to me and placed it in the middle of the room alongside another member of the group. Everyone settled down. Only after events were under way did I fully realise I had not chosen wisely in the chair department. By then, of course, it was much too late to do anything about it. Charles had already started the process of initiation. As I awaited my turn to be attuned to the Reiki energy, I remember quite vividly having to struggle valiantly to sit upright in a very uncomfortable Bentwood chair. The chair was definitely unstable and the positioning of my posterior on it precarious to say the least. One false move or wriggle in the wrong direction could quite easily see me slipping unceremoniously to the floor. There was nothing for it. I just had to reconcile myself to the discomfort and hang on in there. It wasn't easy trying to do that whilst, at the same time, trying not to make a noise and distract others. No matter which way I sought to straighten up and align myself, the narrow unyielding back of the chair proved ruthless in its dedicated determination to brand my shoulder blades with its curved outline. I found it nigh on impossible to concentrate on any part of the initiation. Instead, I tried to focus on deep breathing. Inhale, expand, clear the mind. Perhaps by doing that the pain might somehow be lessened and I could get back on board with the initiations. It was a false hope. Nothing seemed to work. Not even the softness of an old feather cushion could help alleviate my discomfort. It was definitely a distraction I could have done without. No doubt the initiations being carried out by Charles were as inspiring and fascinating as I imagined they would be. All I kept wishing was for Charles to just get a move on and speed things up a bit. My body and I could not take very much more branding. The sooner the chair and I detached ourselves from each other and went our separate ways the better. I longed to stand up and stretch my limbs and bring some form of soothing balm to my protesting, aching back. What a way for an initiate to be introduced to a new energy!

The timing seemed just right for the weekend to reach its inevitable ending. As I look back over those two days, certain elements I had no particular or defining memory of at the time seize their small window of opportunity and determine to resurrect themselves. I give myself permission to go with the flow and remember.

As my friend and I left the magnificence of the copper beeches behind, and pointed her car in an easterly direction and home, a sense of euphoria swept over us. I remember very clearly getting caught up in the moment and laughing a great deal. We chattered and reminisced about the events of the day. The play button connected to language had been pressed and the words continued to keep tumbling out. I do not think we could have stopped talking even supposing we had wanted to.

Ever since we had been attuned we kept expecting our energy levels to dip a little. Because we did not know any better we had somehow convinced ourselves in advance that we would probably feel exhausted after our experiences. In fact, the complete opposite was true. We felt greatly enervated and energised. We found ourselves almost exploding as enormous surges of super-charged adrenalin and feverish excitement coursed through us. There was a silent and unspoken acceptance and knowing that these feelings had absolutely no intention whatsoever of being restricted or contained in any way. The hastily erected barriers put in place for a lifetime would simply deconstruct and crumble into the vast expanse of memory. Time alone would determine the speed at which the new feelings would allow us an insight into their content. We understood that.

The promise of things yet to come was almost unbearable. It had only been a matter of minutes since we left our fellow Reiki students behind, but both of us knew our lives had been irrevocably changed. Now that we had experienced the mystery and wonder of Reiki, we knew we would see and view things from an entirely different perspective. Without being fully able to articulate or understand why, we became consciously aware of another aspect of ourselves. Both of us had a very real sense that somehow, on a physical level, some intrinsic 'thing' had changed. Whether it had or not is of course open to debate. Perhaps it was just the expansion of consciousness. I do know we felt a physical element we previously had no sense of.

As my friend drove she and I tried to imagine what it would be like to become a Reiki master. Initially, we concluded that it would take years and years, perhaps even as many as fifteen years before we could contemplate scaling those particular giddying heights. We pacified ourselves with the thought that there would always be exceptions to the rule. Both of us were greatly encouraged by the fact that Charles had been so young when he became a master. It gave us hope that one day, maybe not too far down the track, we might actually manage to achieve that particular goal. On a more realistic note, we recognised that Reiki was still very much in its infancy and we were effectively still infant scholars.

Our acceptance of being the new kids on the block as far as Reiki was concerned did not, in our eyes, curb or limit our intention or desire to explore other avenues of spiritual interest. No sooner had we just taken our first tentative steps, and already we found ourselves wanting something more. We were amused at the giant leaps forward we were making in our minds. Had we learnt nothing over the weekend about walking the spiritual path? Well, we had and we had not. I think it was a perfectly natural and understandable reaction to feel impatient. Of course, we didn't just want to walk the path. We were inspired, and full of so much optimism about our futures, we wanted to run as fast as our legs could carry us and go straight to the finish line. Neither of us wanted to wait for the next instalment of our lives, even though we knew in reality we would have to.

When my friend dropped me off and headed home I felt high as a kite. My head was spinning. Every nerve ending was jingling and jangling, every light in my head flashing. I found it difficult to hone in and focus on any one thing. A few random thoughts did eventually decide to help me out and attempted to rally to the flag, but the thoughts were so frenetic and impossible to grasp. Just as soon as they made an appearance, they quickly evaporated again. Because it probably was meant, nothing registered with any degree of permanency.

As I struggled to take control of my thoughts one thing started to slowly filter through into my consciousness. Accompanying the initial emergence of Reiki knowledge was the unwavering belief and understanding that some profound thing inside me had definitely been kick-started. It was not purely an acceptance of that in a physical sense. It sounds slightly contradictory, but there was an inner knowingness in the spiritual sense, yet this knowingness was still hard to fathom. That realisation was not just like the dawning of another new day for me, but the dawning of a new life. Some may find it fanciful for me to be saying this, but the reality was I don't think I had ever felt more alive than I did at that moment. I was so much more aware on so many different levels than I had ever been before. Channelling my thoughts might be proving difficult, but my intuition and sense of knowing was showing me and letting me know that some seismic cosmic shift in my consciousness had definitely taken place. What I chose to do with that was entirely up to me.

The silence of the house hit me as soon as I opened the front door. Like a favourite garment it slipped effortlessly over me. I was grateful for that familiar embrace and the sense of comfort it brought. Familiar was what was needed. My whole body was tingling with energy almost to the point of agitation. A sense of calm being restored was what I really needed. This was much easier said than done. I could tell pretty well straight away that that was not about to happen any time soon. The word calm seemed to have distanced itself from my disorderly thought process.

If I couldn't find the calm I so desperately sought then some other course of action would be needed. In order to remove myself from the noisy distractions of the mind, I decided what would benefit me most was to stretch out in my old blue recliner and just try to relax. Some jasmine tea from my favourite china breakfast cup would help the process along. Even that turned out to be a struggle. The constant, flowing stream of dialogue and mindless chit chat, trying so very hard not to be mindless, become a serious irritant. I had to do something to take things down a notch or two and help me feel just a little bit more balanced and less out of sync with myself. For my own sanity and peace of mind I knew I had to get it together. The sooner that happened then the happier I would be. No sooner had I thought that than I decided to totally disregard my own advice. Although my need to feel more balanced was overriding everything else I knew, I could not force things along. No matter how much I tried, it just was not going to happen. As seconds, then minutes, passed me by I quickly sensed that marching to my own directional tune and drumbeat wasn't an alternative open to me. I came to the slow realisation that, irrespective of the ceaseless questioning and uncontrollable agitation, everything I was experiencing was just as it should be.

As the evening progressed, and the immediacy of seeking balance and calm slackened its grip a little, I could sense the urgency to think return. The need was so great I found myself almost wanting to force the issue to think. I soon discovered, however, that whilst thinking was obviously possible, I could not think with any real degree of clarity. There were still so many thoughts wrestling and struggling to get some sort of foothold. All of them were trying to gain an advantage and find a safe place to land.

Everything was such a jumble, and I had the oddest sensation of something really strange going on inside my head. Ridiculous as I know this will sound to others, I sensed my head begin to expand. As a result, it felt twenty or thirty times its normal size. Of course, I realise the sheer madness and impossibility of such a thing happening, BUT the sensation I was experiencing felt very real to me. It was impossible to avoid giving recognition to this moment of ludicrous and humorous distraction. I should really have done what I wanted to do, and that was to laugh out loud at the absurdity of the situation. Should have and could have.... yet I did not.

Further ridiculous imagery immediately began to surface and float slowly, like softened downy clouds, right across the path of my consciousness. Instead of disregarding the imagery, I found myself totally absorbed and giving it time, brain space and recognition. The content of the thought may have been nonsensical, but at least it was clear, individual thought and not quite so jumbled anymore.

Progressing rapidly into the realms of silliness, I gave free rein to the image of my tiny body supporting the weight of my new oversized head. Amusing as the image was, I did wonder at one point if I should really be encouraging this mind play to continue. I suppose in the end curiosity got the better of me, and I allowed myself to linger in the craziness a little longer.

When the question arose I knew it needed addressing. As I assimilated the prodigious amount of information and knowledge being downloaded from the universe, would the capacity of my head prove adequate, or would it have to continue to expand even more? Indulging and stepping further into my own silliness, I began to wonder if it was beyond the realms of possibility that my head might actually explode, or failing that, implode into thousands of tiny shattered particles. Would I ever be whole again? I wondered. From the sleepy recesses of my brain a continuous loop of surreal Monty Python-type scenarios rose in instant comedic flashbacks. The images were so hilarious and fantastical and just kept on coming. There was nothing else for it. I gave myself over to what I was feeling inside and started to giggle uncontrollably. It was just the release I needed.

Eventually, the laughter and silliness subsided. Sanity, if that is what it is called, was more or less restored. Although the initial mind confusion had relented significantly, it still refused to yield absolutely. Instead of leaving things as they were, I tried again to take control and completely still my mind. It was not successful. My mind was not for stilling. Not then anyway, and, as it was to turn out, not for quite some time to come.

post weekend

Over the next few days, a certain degree of serenity and calmness was eventually restored. This only happened as a result of a great deal of reflection and not so quiet contemplation. As I trawled and heaved my way through a review of my life, I could see it with an honesty I had probably never owned up or admitted to before. I could and did accept that my life had been a good life, filled with many incredible blessings, for which I could be thankful and extremely grateful. Although I had not always expressed my gratitude, or given voice to those thanks, I knew in my head and my heart I was particularly blessed. The only real problem I was having with that was I just was not entirely sure to whom I should be offering thanks for all these blessings. Knowing my history as far as God was concerned, could I or should I in all good consciousness be offering thanks to him?

Throughout most of my life I had been having an on-off relationship with God. I had alternated between being a believer in my youth to being not quite so believing when my twenties and early thirties sprinted by. Currently, my relationship was in off mode. Whilst issues or things were not really resolved between God and myself as far as any belief I might, or might not have about his existence, after the weekend I did concede to feeling 'something' I had not felt before. I am not saying that a Reiki weekend was responsible for making me aware of the possibility or permanent occupancy in my life of a God, but some core thing shifted within me. Even though I was reluctant to be having this conversation with myself right at that moment, I resigned myself to the kicking off again of further internal discussions about God. Right there and then, I made the decision not to fight with myself over God anymore. Enough of that had been done in the past. As if to honour that decision, after the events of the weekend I stated my intention to consciously give thanks for every single day of my life from then on in.

Just when I thought I was making progress and advancing, the past reared up once more and led me into a period of further reflection. Reflection is such a difficult thing to budge once it has taken hold. I longed to move forward and deflect these reflections, and confine them to the past, but the past was not yet ready to give way, and still knocked firmly at the door. Reluctantly, there was little or no alternative. I had to open the door a fraction and allow that past in again. Hopefully, it would be a brief visitation.

As the slide-show began my participation was as inevitable as it was mandatory. Images from the slides remind me there had certainly been some pretty serious ups and downs along the road I had mapped out for myself. There was no denying the fact that I had been fortunate in life. A quick review of events determined that there had been more ups than downs. That was not to say that I had managed to circumnavigate my way through life unscathed. There were scars both visible and invisible. Some of the scars ran long and deep. These were the ones that had the greatest impact and the most profound effect on the choices I made in relation to the living of my life. Early in my thirties, I discovered what it was like to be and feel alone and apart from the very persons whose lives I longed so desperately to be a part of. I encountered long periods when I thought loneliness would swallow me up and devour me. Living was not always easy.

Spotting the chink in the chain of reflection, the acute feelings of isolation and being cut adrift, which had so affected parts of my life in the past, chose that exact moment to try and infiltrate and resurrect themselves. They did not succeed in their mission. I was not about to grant admission or permission and let those thoughts sneak back in and destroy the newly found senses and feelings of being part of something bigger. Instantly, the thoughts began to dissolve and melt away. In my heart of hearts I instinctively knew that the occasional rogue thought and sense of loneliness could and would still creep up on me and catch me at any weakened moment of its choosing. The thought of that happening did not fill me with the same sense of dread as it would have in the past. Instead, I was just happy and elated to finally be rid of the source of so many of these negative thoughts and sensations. Relegating these reflections to the sidelines of my history almost left me feeling slightly victorious somehow. This surely was cause for celebration.

I no longer had the lingering sense of being so alone. The reality for me was I had become a part of this amazing new worldwide club of people who had a common shared experience. In discovering more about myself, and what I needed to do to sustain myself, a new, more evolved me emerged. If I listened to what my heart was telling me I would never ever really be apart from life again. Knowing and understanding this reality felt as incredible as it was.

The years which immediately followed that first weekend were amazing. I had always known they would be revelatory. It took a lot longer than I thought it would, but eventually I regained control over the runaway section of my brain. Life began to settle down again. I could say that some form of normality returned, but that would not be true. I never sought or wanted normality, per se. I wanted a life that would be everything it was supposed to be, and so much more besides. It did take me some time to stop feeling quite so guilty for wanting all of that for myself, but then I realised there was nothing wrong at all in wanting more for oneself. I stopped beating myself about it.

As I set the course for my future, I took the time to reflect on just how much my life had changed for the better. Although I was keen to avoid making comparisons, some of the everyday experiences from the second part of my life were already proving much more positive experiences than the first part. Things were different. I was different. Life still had its ups and downs, but that was just life. It was the same for everyone. The real changes came in the way I chose to see my life and the way in which I chose to live it. It also came down to the choices I made for myself. I had a responsibility to myself. It was no longer good enough just to make the choices. I had to make sure all my choices were informed choices. That way, I only had myself to blame if things went pear-shaped.

Being more spiritually aware and better able to deal with certain aspects of my life definitely had its advantages. It helped me cope with the very real changes taking place in my life. I found myself being challenged and stretched at almost every turn. Everything in my life began to pick up pace. I determined to re evaluate my entire life. No easy task, I told myself. In the past I had let my life unfold and evolve of its own accord. On the whole it had followed the path I had set out for it. At the time I had not consciously asked myself whether this was a good thing or a bad thing. I just accepted it was what it was. I do not honestly think I was even aware enough to give living much more than a thought in the passing of the day. There was certainly no element or defining recognition of life being the gift it was. Instead, it was just an acceptance of living a life. It is only now, reflecting on those memories that I am able to admit to myself that

I was probably far too caught up in my own life and its insignificant dramas. I say insignificant but I know at the time of experiencing the dramas it probably didn't feel like that. Time and reflection are master teachers and definitely change the way we view events.

If a bigger picture existed I probably did not even recognise it, let alone acknowledge it. Though I really hope this was not the case, I was probably too engrossed with myself and what was taking place in my own limiting little world. Was the reality of my life really so limiting or is memory playing advocate here? The people inhabiting my life were obviously participating freely in it, but perhaps I made things difficult for myself by thinking of myself purely as a participant passing through. Who knows? During that specific period of my life I simply cannot remember now what my views on life and living were. If I had any defining life altering views then they possibly were not true to their word and I have forgotten them.

At some level I recognise I had had a conscious awareness of living and been aware of the consciousness of living, but I can now accept that it was not a full-blown consciousness. I had been actively responsible for the content and living part of my life. At the end of the day, it was still just a part-contribution. Certain important elements and spiritual truths were missing, and I did not have all the facts to hand. If I had that might have enabled me to make better choices and, as a result, led me to a more enriched and fulfilled life. I find myself instantly irritated by my words. They are a shallow and total misrepresentation of my truth. My life is not, has not and will not be a life of 'if only'. For me, the most important things are the choices I make about my life now and in my future. They are the only ones I have input to and any sort of control over. They are the only ones which will really matter to me as I go about living my life from a place of Truth.

Extract no. 2:
Mother nature's poppies —
Summer 1992

I sense the exact moment the culmination of my nightly workings amongst the stars and nocturnal journeying through the galaxies comes to its inevitable gentle parting. Before my body can completely reintegrate and realign itself with daytime mode, my mind registers the fact that something novel is occurring. For the second day in succession, the sun is shining.

As I give myself over to thoughts and promises of the day ahead, my senses are awakened to the joy of it all. With marginal assistance from my elbows, I prop myself up and allow my head to fall gently again into the soft indentations of the pillows. In a state of complete stillness I watch brilliant shafts of early morning sunlight bounce randomly off the picture frame windows, spinning and tracing their delicate rainbow imagery on to the ceiling above me. In those first few moments I instinctively know there would be no more teasing of a summer in the offing. The long awaited days have finally arrived.

In an instant, the internal barometer governing my feel good factor swiftly rises by several degrees. Instead of the cursory, eyes straightforward, silent greeting normally heralding the start of my daylight hours, I find myself smiling, delighted at the prospect of the day ahead. Immediately, all is well within the parameters of my world. I take the time to savour the moment and accept that today is going to be a good day! With Mother Nature so generous in her provision, I hope I can look forward to a summer full of just such days.

Something seemingly as simple as the rays of the sun reaching out to touch me always did, and still does, invoke the same reactions within me. When the sun decides to grace the skies and show her face, an internal, mood enhancer trigger is activated from deep inside. In an instant, the entire outcome of the day is altered for the better.

Automatically, I sense my sluggish spirits splutter, then surge. Letting go, and handing myself over to just experiencing a sensation like that, is a wonderfully liberating feeling and one I give free rein to. It has been a long time coming around. All through the dark winter months I have run with my natural instinct and allowed such feelings of simplistic sun-fuelled exhilaration to go into shutdown mode. It is time to reactivate the senses from their slumbering hibernation and turn my face towards the sunlight once more. I feel happy knowing that new life experiences to add to my ever-expanding memory bank lie but a breath away.

With memories returning, so too do the thoughts of living in the day nature has presented me. I have lost track of the number of times I have forgotten the act of honouring the day and the joys and blessings that filter into the living of such a day. In my haste to get on with what is around the next corner, I am as guilty as any when it comes to taking things for granted and ignoring the moment. As I rush full pelt towards the next experience, I forget to just stop and live in the experience of the moment.

All of us need to be reminded occasionally that natural occurrences in the calendar of life can often trigger the greatest rewards. We should remember more often how timeless and effortless it is to embrace the beauty and simplicity of living in the joy of the moment. How often are we reminded to do just that? How often do we listen and take on board that advice? Sadly, the answer to both questions is either seldom, or not enough. As I rise and look out upon the open countryside before me, I give more thought to the actual moment I am standing in. I relax at the sight and sound of nature and the glorious living gift she has so generously and selflessly bestowed upon me. I try tuning into my surroundings, but find my whole thought process more than a little askew. Tripping and tumbling in an erratic type of free fall, it is heading straight towards the centre of a rapidly expanding, spiralling vortex. Amidst this minor mind confusion, I somehow regain a little control and manage to partially still my thoughts. Large blocks and debris have manifested out of nowhere and threaten to block my advancement. I begin the task of dismantling them. It is a relatively easy undertaking and is completed in no time at all. The next challenge I must tackle finds me concentrating on releasing the persistent babble and constant mind chatter swirling around inside my head. This simple act helps me hone in and focus on the present. Mind calmed and thoughts now stilled, it is not so difficult engaging and focusing on the beauty and heartbeat of all that surrounds me. My heart skips an excited beat or two of its own as it settles into a sunny, celebratory mode.

I decide to give some of my more mundane daily tasks a miss. Days like today have of late been few and far between in my neck of the woods. Instead of my usual solitary breakfast at the dining table, I determine to go into the garden and have breakfast surrounded by nature. The decision to just enjoy the day is an easy one. A couple of months ago I certainly would not have been able to do this without revisiting the pages and making a trip into my memory bank. That is the thing about consciously living in the gift nature decides to present us with. We may think we can, but even as the seasons come and go, none of us can accurately predict or pre-determine what that gift will be. It is that very unpredictability which keeps all of us alert and on our toes, and makes life the exciting journey it is. One never really knows what to expect. Because of its vagaries, and sometimes just because it can, nature unsettles the rhythm of life and the living of it. In case any of us should forget the extent of her reach, nature will throw the odd curved ball or two to jog our memories and remind us of her existence. She is a constant in all our lives and in a heartbeat can transform the ordinary into the extraordinary.

My memory lingers a second or two longer and does another spot of its own traversing. I am reminded that perhaps if the seasons had been a little kinder, and we had not experienced such a bitter winter or prolonged earth sodden spring, we might have allowed ourselves to slip into that comfortable space in our head where familiar expectancy is the norm. Nature might have followed its annual course of progression. The first rays of summer could easily have slipped under the radar without any nod of acknowledgement. Because my expectations from nature did not materialise as I had anticipated, by the time yesterday and today came around I was much more aware of my connection with nature and the feeling of quiet expectancy within me. Creating the energy around the thought of a sun-filled day assists in the possibility of that day materialising. Once again, I am reminded of just how much I take for granted in life and determine to try not to.

I take up residence on the long, stone bench in the garden and let the silence and sound of my surroundings wrap around me. I am not conscious of thinking about anything specific. In the midst of this enveloping stillness, I sense words begin to take form. They feel like an intrusion I could do without. Out of nowhere the phrases about 'everything being in the hands of the gods' and/or 'reaping what one sows' pop up. Just in case I had somehow forgotten, they flash a reminder. I find myself distracted a little at the timing of this, but as the questions have presented themselves for a reason, I pause and give the phrases the time they have requested. Although I have just de-cluttered my mind, I feel gentle stirrings as the recently vacated space gears up in response to the questions now slowly taking shape. I allow the thoughts to formulate and take me where they will.

Regardless of one's belief system, be it god-like or not, our own understanding of the reality of natural life and the living of it is what it is...or is not. All of it is dependant on the individual concerned and the actions they take, and the decisions they make, either towards or resulting from that. In any case, I ask myself what qualifies as reality or REAL life. Is life REAL or is it just an illusionary physical 'something' put in place to give credence to structure of thought and present us with a sense of life and living? To some, the very use of the word REAL might infer, or give rise to, the suggestion that there is another life which is NOT real. Is that NOT real world another form of reality? What constitutes reality to one person might, in the reality of another person, be something entirely different. Instead of just living their lives, many people have a tendency to over think and get bogged down with theorising life. They spend a large part of their lives interpreting and trying to understand life. By indulging themselves in too much navel gazing and introspection they make their lives and living far more complicated than it needs to be. When it comes right down to it, our own singular interpretation of what IS REAL is the only one we can live our lives around. Life and living is dictated by the circumstances of a given situation and the ensuing choices we make in regard to that situation. There is no one else who can do that for us. We have sole, as well as soul, responsibility governing the very breadth of the choices we decide to make for ourselves. Others can participate and have direct input into the journey of our life, but we ultimately have the final say as to the outcome.

Seeking any sort of guidance on REAL life is not as easy as one might think. Whom do you turn to and whom do you ask to help bring you the clarity you seek? If you decide to go down the road others have taken and seek their viewpoint on reality, whilst it will no doubt be informative, you might find yourself being short-changed and a little disappointed. As far as I am aware, there is no definitive guide or handbook on the reality of living in a REAL world. Hundreds, if not thousands, of books have been written on the meaning of life, but how many leave you with a feeling of really getting to the central core of understanding as it pertains to your life and the world you inhabit? Do you know anyone out there who has mastered the art of living in the reality of a REAL world? Many are of the mind that there is no such thing as reality. I am not sure I agree, disagree or even pretend to fully understand that whole concept. I hear the words alright, but what do they mean in order for them to have meaning and reality for me?

I return to the god/s and the idea of my life being in his/their hands. How much truth or accuracy is there in that statement? Though the narrative in my head is a little disjointed, I proceed with my meanderings. I ask this question of myself; do I believe that my life is my own, or is it genuinely a case of my life really being in the hands of gods? Is my life, and the living of it, therefore an equal partnership between myself and the gods, or do the gods play a much greater role in my life than I have previously given them credit for? The internal dialogue in my head advances as additional thoughts on god/s' participation in my life begin to emerge. I ask these questions of myself: is my commitment to my life lesser than the gods' commitment to my life?; do I want that to be the case and is it something I believe to be true?; is it something I actively seek?; do I even know if I can relate to the existence of gods in my world? I think about this, and though I conclude that I might be open to the concept of gods in my life, I am not wholly convinced. Different cultures have very different belief systems. The majority of people around the world have an understanding of the term gods as far as it relates to them. Many will have their own idea of who their gods are.

Some will pay homage to their gods, whilst others openly worship at the feet of their gods. Others prefer to communicate and honour their gods in a quieter fashion. There are others who do not believe that any gods in any form exist. Regardless of which religion one might believe in, and what gods one acknowledges there is in existence, a common thread of Faith that binds us all to one another. That can only give us all leave to celebrate.

Over the years my questioning has led me to believe in a singular energy I call Source. If I am to be entirely truthful about the word god I recognise it has not always sat comfortably with me. I do use the word god, just not as often as I use the word Source. To avoid any confusion concerning the extracts from my journal, I decide that since I have been writing about gods I will continue to use the name God. I am not convinced about using the plural term of the word as it relates to my life so will stick with the singular.

Further thoughts of my life and God emerge. These are not smooth, everyday thoughts. They are prickly and refuse to be negated or marginalised. Why at times is God such a struggle for me? Would it be regarded as frivolous and an act of indirect blasphemy I wonder if I allow my mind to think in terms of percentages and who is the greatest contributor to my life? Is it God or myself? At the end of the day does it really matter? Who would know anyway, apart from me and God? What difference would knowing the answer make in the grand scheme of things? I consider if the idea of a life not entirely one hundred per cent under the auspices of my own control is something I can readily acknowledge or accept? Do I want to? Do I feel the need to? Do I actually believe that anyway?

What I am a believer in is predestination. Although I might have come late to that realisation, when it happened my acceptance was absolute. I truly believe that the choices I make in connection with my lifetime on the earthly plane are paramount in helping determine the entire outcome of my life. Long before that minuscule spark, which is me, broke away from the source, which is God, and came into this world, the decision about whom exactly my parents would be and how my life would turn out had already been decided upon. By virtue of my belief in God, that very same tiny spark which would transform itself into me is responsible for that. I ask myself if I have done a good job with my life, or have I got it all horribly wrong? What, if any, are the lessons to be learnt from my experiences? Even supposing it is possible, would I want to change things around somehow, or is there a quiet acceptance and understanding of the choices I have made and the way my life has turned out? Is this the life I have so purposefully and intentionally chosen for myself? Given those choices again, would I opt for a completely different set of experiences and their subsequent outcomes?

As I ask myself what lessons have been learnt whilst I journeyed through my life, I wonder if unresolved issues of this lifetime would continue and carry over into another of my coming lifetimes? The question threw me a little because I thought I already knew the answer to it. Past experience has certainly indicated that, until the lesson is learnt and understood, it would continue to crop up again in another lifetime. I believe that. There have definitely been times along the way when I have questioned myself about the wisdom of the things I chose to experience. If I had known in advance about the many hardships, disappointments, pain, suffering, and the removal from my life of a healthy body, would I consciously have made the choices I so clearly did? Why would someone make the decision to experience such things when life could be made so much easier and a whole lot less problematical? Some may find it difficult to believe me when I say I wouldn't change anything. My choices would remain the same. So many people on Earth have similar experiences to mine in life. It is called living. My trials and tribulations are no lesser or greater than the vast majority of the general public. On reflection, I have been luckier than most with my predestined life.

To my way of thinking, if one believes in predestination it follows that one accepts a consciousness before conception. Not everyone can get their head around that and take it on board. Perhaps one's real birth should be seen as the exact moment the spark of us started its journey? Did I trigger that spark or did God, or did my parents own sparks all those years ago actually trigger the whole chain of events? I think what I am trying to say is this; if I did not believe in the existence of God there would be no spark in the first place. As a result of that there would be no me. God and I exist because of each other's contribution to life. His consciousness lives in me and through me. There is no separation. God is representative of the whole, and I am part of that whole.

Once again I ask myself the God questions. Is the issue of my life being in my hands or out of my hands resolved? Also, is their any truth in reaping what I sow? Instead of resolution to this, another question is raised. I follow the question with little or no expectation of where it might lead.

If, as individuals, we travel our path through life trying to live that life from a place of Grace and understanding, does that make us less likely to attract the attention of God or more likely, or doesn't it make any difference at all? Are negative factors less likely to come into our lives as a result of an openly loving and giving heart? Do we attract fewer disastrous events purely because we live in that state of Grace? If we encourage and endeavour to make the world better and more aware of the incredible opportunities we have been gifted, do those very acts mark us out for special treatment in the eyes of God? Does being proactive and contributing to the nurturing of the world help us as individuals stand out for some form of preferential treatment? Do we find ourselves living with a sense of entitlement because of the things we do? Do we do things with conscious expectation of reward, or is the act of giving enough? Should we even think in terms of any reward at all?

I have always thought that reaping what one sows has negative connotations. In reality, it is some form of punishment for those who have done harm to others. It goes hand-in-hand with the saying of what goes around, comes around. That last statement about things coming around has always slightly irritated me. Who came up with that one, and how much truth is there in that anyway? Whilst some might find solace and comfort in the idea of redressing injustices done, does it really help to have some type of payback? Will it bring solace and comfort to the injured party? In the sense of bringing peace back to your heart, is the retaliatory road one you would wish to go down? Will it somehow alter the chain of events leading to the initial injustice? Can the painful, damaged void be repaired by dishing out one's own punishment in return? How does seeking retribution in any way enrich one's life? If you think that justice can only be served by punishing the protagonist, then perhaps it is time to seek an alternative thought process. Many people might have reservations and doubts about a non-reactionary stance being the great panacea in redressing the injured balance. There still remain many ways in which justice can be served without reverting to acts of aggression.

In the case of reaping what one sows, perhaps after a lifetime of believing in the negative aspects associated with the above statement, I should instead give some consideration to the fact that I have it back to front and it actually means the exact opposite. The words really mean one is rewarded for the apparent good one does. From where I am standing, I don't feel I want to give any energy to that whole reaping and rewarding thing. I would much rather just get on with the doing thing.

I once knew someone who stated that there was no such thing as an unselfish act. One of the examples used was even the act of giving could be seen as selfish because, not only did it make one feel good about the giving, it also made one feel good about oneself in return. At the time I felt saddened by what I saw as the cynicism of the statement. That person was not for budging. For every example to the contrary, so that example was negated in the eyes of that person. I gave thought to the person's view and in time the view was tucked away in the recesses of my mind. Until fairly recently that is. I cannot remember the circumstance, but something caused its re-emergence. I found myself wondering if I still held onto the same belief system I had back then or had my viewpoint changed in the intervening period? I thought I felt the same way, yet I found myself doubting. Was the statement about the act being unselfish a sweeping generalisation, or did it hold any vestige of truth? Did people in general do good in order to be seen as good and not for the simple act of doing? Had life really been reduced to that degree of self-absorption? Were people really so cynical and calculating? Surely that could not be the case, could it? Whatever happened to the spontaneous gesture, or acting on the impulse of the moment? No thought of payback of any kind, just the simple pleasure of giving. There couldn't really be any selfish act attached to that, could there? Though I still believed in the propensity for people to do what they believe is the right and selfless thing, I found my viewpoint had shifted slightly. Reluctantly, I came to the realisation, unpalatable though it was, that we were now living in part in a world where image had taken precedence over many aspects of people's lives. This great silent invader had crept up on us all without anyone really noticing. Before we knew where we were, image had firmly rooted itself in our psyche.

As a result of this some sections of society had become immersed in the whole image and doing thing, and separated from much of what once made them feel good about living their lives. They began to worry too much about how they were perceived by others. Whilst it was not necessarily the case for the vast majority, many craved recognition and plaudits for doing something that previously would have been given freely from the heart. Are you open to acknowledging or accepting that there may be some truth in my words? Have you at some time or another gone down that particular self-congratulatory road in search of similar plaudits? Did you see something on that road you recognised? Did it make you feel as though you were a part of something, or apart from everything? Did you seek to portray an image of yourself as some type of munificent benefactor? If that was the case, then, if you feel it is appropriate, perhaps you might want to ask yourself why. If you have not already done so, then ask yourself now if this is the road you still wish to travel upon, or is it time to make fresh inroads and find your real self again? Without the need for too much introspection, wouldn't life be so much better for all if we decided to pare back and live from a place of Truth and Love again, and not from a place where image rules and expectant reward becomes the norm?

Even if it is only for a moment, please stop and give a little thought to the words I have just written. Do any of them resonate with you? What are your views on the questions posed? Do you hold any specific views in response? Do you occasionally wish your life could be simpler, more loving, more truthful? Should less emphasis be placed on image and more on giving? Are you fortunate enough to already have found your place in the grand scheme of things and be living your life from a place of Grace and Truth? If this is the case for you, then you are one of the truly blessed.

All of us view life through different lenses and perspectives. This is a good thing. Allow yourself to think about this for a moment or two then ask this question; is there room for improvement in the way you choose to live your life? Do you want to, or even feel the need to? I know what my response to that question is. Every day, I try to make that day better than the day before. Every day, I try to make the world I inhabit a better world by trying to make a difference, no matter how small it might be. Something as simple as a smile which acknowledges the existence of someone whose path you cross might make all the difference in the world to that particular person. That one small act of recognition may help remove the cloak of isolation and invisibility and lift that person from the darkness of their world into a new day where the light shines upon them. Such a simple little thing can be effective and life changing without us even knowing it. I make the conscious decision every single day to be more accepting of others and more giving of myself and, though I do not always succeed, I do always try.

My thoughts return to individuals and their interpretation of the way they see their lives. I do not believe it is either necessary or essential for everyone to be of one mind, coming from the same page. Diversity of opinion is healthy. It helps stimulate thought, and helps the universe to keep breathing and evolving. Previously, I stated my belief in predestination. I also believe there are aspects of our lives where we have little or no control over what God or Mother Nature decides should come our way. Should both decide to be gentle in their treatment of us, then we should feel nurtured and blessed. Let me return briefly to the topic of reward. If ever one did find oneself thinking of reward of any kind then surely the nurture and blessings from God and Mother Nature would be more than enough to eclipse any material sense of reward?

I have almost forgotten that I started off this day by celebrating the gift from nature's treasure chest. Along the way I have digressed a great deal. I have indulged myself and my wandering thoughts. It is far too late now to employ the diversionary tactics I perhaps could have, had I really wanted to. The old maxim of never say never is one I can stand by. I focus my mind and return to the original thoughts of the day.

In the opening paragraph of these extracts I speak about nature and honouring her. More often than not what we perceive as apparent downturns in nature's giving can often be counteracted by an upturn as nature seeks to redress the balance. The comparisons between nature and the life we live are there for all to see. It does not skirt around the edges any more. It is at the front of our consciousness. That has never been more apparent than over the last decade or so. Every time we turn on the news or read a newspaper these days the headlines scream out with words and images of the latest drought or flood or earthquake. Ecological, environmental and climatic disasters have become the norm and seem to face us at every turn. If that was not enough of an attention grabber, our conscience kicks in and rightly reminds us that we have a duty to this planet to face up to and try to address the reality of man made catastrophes. It is a foolish person who decides to take a back seat when disaster strikes around the world. Ignore Mother Nature at your peril. The majority of people try to acknowledge and commit to doing their 'bit' to deal with events which unsettle and replace them with balance. From my own perspective there has really been little to complain or grumble about. Because she is nature's natural provider Mother Earth hands out her yearly offerings. Sometimes, these are seen as incredible gifts and blessings. Other times, they can seem less so. As recipients, we should be gracious in our acceptance. All are blessings to be taken on board and experienced.

Once again, my eyes begin to scan the beautiful rolling countryside surrounding the village I call home. No matter what the season, or how often I look upon this particular view, it never disappoints. I notice how over a period of just a few days the landscape has altered quite considerably. The seemingly endless expanse and shock of intense colour of the once vibrant, blooming, early oil seed rape fields has begun to fade a little. By way of compensation, acres of green summer crops have now turned their faces towards the promise of a ripening yet to come. All along the edges of the fields, wayward shoots of floral colours struggle to find a way through the tangled roots and weeds as Mother Nature coaxes her wards ever upwards to a glorious sun-filled life.

A sense of wellbeing washes over me as I reminisce about a summer many years ago. I had moved out of the city into a pretty little village hugging a secluded position along the coastal path. The location of my old stone cottage on the very edge of the village was idyllic. The proportions of the garden were minuscule compared to others I had nurtured over the years, but nonetheless beautiful for that. The heady mix of the fragrances, and the incredible profusion of colourful plants, really were true wonders to behold. Every individual flower gave so generously and provided me with my own little piece of heaven on Earth. That particular year the poppies were magnificent and also extremely prolific. As the summer months progressed, I began to realise I wasn't just running out of space for the inevitable replanting of the surplus poppy seeds, I had run out of space entirely. I had given away so many plants over the years to various friends, but unfortunately they also had run out of space for any additional plantings.

Mother Nature had been so magnanimous I knew I had to honour her and try to do something in return for her. When the planting season came around again I collected all the dried -over -winter seed heads from the poppies and determined to find a suitable place to plant them. Where better I thought than on the overgrown grassy verge opposite my rickety old garden gate? Shouldn't everyone have the same opportunity to celebrate the beauty of nature that had so benefited me?

It took time and a lot of hard work to clear the area and finally scatter those seeds. I declared my intention for a successful outcome. As I planted my own little seeds of hope, I struck up an internal dialogue with them. I blessed them and asked them to help me gift nature by growing tall and strong and beautiful. I asked them to help me transform a barren patch of earth into a glorious display of colour and movement. To my amazement, practically all the seeds germinated and started to create a young but strong root system. By the time the summer months came along again the entire length of the verge was covered in poppies bursting through the rich dark soil. That first year the display of poppies was spectacular. It was nothing compared to the following years, however. With wonderful precision timing the first verdant shoots would force their way through the darkened surface of the dense, uneven soil. This was normally followed in rapid succession by incredible spurts of growth. One or two flower heads would appear and exhibit their tight bulbous promise. They were painstakingly slow in revealing the first slender hint of colour. By the time all the poppies had fully opened the entire stretch of roadside verge was awash with ramrod straight sentinels bearing glorious, pillar-box red petals and the blackest of black centres. As the eye-catching display continued to enthral and flourish, people would stop and look at this amazing spectacle. As the years went by photographers would make annual pilgrimages to capture the beauty of those poppies. Recently, on a trip to the beach, I passed my old cottage. My heart gave an extra beat of wonderment. That simple act all that time ago was still bringing joy into the lives of others. The poppies were still standing tall, still being admired and still doing honour to Mother Nature in all her graciousness.

Wouldn't it be amazing if we could all scatter a few more seeds of hope? It really would not require much effort on our behalf. The seeds don't even have to be floral. They can be universal; a kindly deed, a thoughtful word, a listening, hearing ear. The simplest acts can have the biggest impact, just as long as they come from your heart.

After the heavenly day, the hours of early evening beckon and reach out to embrace me. I am back now in the present, in the moment. My mind has stilled again and I am at peace with myself and with my world. I have no desires or needs, other than the reality of now. All is exactly as it should be. My great benefactor, the sun, has blessed me with a truly beautiful day, and I am all the more blessed for that. Just as the day has started, so it will end. I smile again in recognition and gratitude.

Extract no. 3:
Preben et al, Special moments in time, Native American drum journeys

Some people see life as a gift; others do not. A small percentage of those who have yet to make up their minds may make a nod in partial acknowledgement. Many more give the entire concept little thought at all. Although variance and division on this topic exists, there is no definitive demarcation line of separation. When it comes down to it, each individual must make their own decision on whether it is a gift or it isn't. I don't think I ever doubt or fail to see the truth of the word or understand its meaning to me. On a personal level I place myself firmly with the 'life is very definitely a gift' camp. Surely there can be nothing more exhilarating and extraordinary than life itself unfolding. It has to be the greatest phenomenon of all time.

By declaring my stance I attach no element of censor or judgement upon any one person or the outcome of their decision-making. At the end of the day, the written word in this extract is just a singular example of my own simple, reflective observations that have accumulated as I have traversed my life. These musings of mine generally tend to be random, but not always. Some have more meaning and substance than others and will take up residency in the foundations of my living. These are the ones that sustain me on many levels of my life and keep me moving forward. I never knowingly choose to ignore experiencing the living of life. Rather than looking at life and its living as something to be endured and to get through, I choose to embrace it. I view this precious gift of life as an exquisite and ever-expanding, intricate patchwork of experiences sewn together with threads of connection and predestination and love. Opportunity is a constant reminder of self-evolution. It arises and enhances and establishes permanence in the overall picture which is my life.

Most of the people I know make the choice to acknowledge and learn from their life experiences before moving onto the next instalment. I am not so very different to anyone else. It took time for me to shake off the inertia of contented acceptance and easy living that occupied the first thirty years of my life. When I realised that change was not only necessary but also inevitable, I prepared myself to jump aboard the greatest magical mystery tour of my entire life. I opened my mind and my heart, and joined like-minded wandering souls in search of new, more meaningful experiences. The journey did not disappoint. It turned out to be the craziest and most spellbinding adventure. Along the way I was blessed to meet many amazing characters, each with a story to tell or with precious memories and information to impart. Experiences were shared. Many were life-changing and left lasting, indelible memories of their own.

What I write about now is one such experience. Every aspect of the experience is so full of Grace and beauty and other extraordinary acts of selfless giving, it cannot fail to secure a very special place in my memory bank and also in my heart. The person responsible for creating and gifting me such a unique experience probably has no awareness how valued and memorable both he and the experience are to me. Before I go directly to the experience, indulge me if you will in a short lead up to the event.

I first heard of Preben through a friend of mine. Although my knowledge of him was scant at best, I can remember from the very outset being intrigued by stories about him. It did not take much persuading for my own intuitive senses to drive me forward and help steer me on the path towards him. Deep down I knew I had to meet this man and get to know him. Whenever anyone spoke of him they always had a rather wistful look or smile on their faces. I liked that. Several regarded him as a spiritual mentor and a bit of a mystic. Whilst I am always a little reluctant to use the word healer, a great number of people determined he had the ability to heal.

Even before I had the opportunity to meet him, in my mind the man had established himself as a bit of an enigma. Stories of his drum workshops and flute playing were legendary and preceded him wherever he chose to go. In the short time since he had taken up residency in Scotland he had built up quite a following. There was an inevitability and unspoken acceptance that our paths would cross sooner rather than later. That was exactly what happened.

All these years later the memory of the first time I see him is still clear. In a group situation, rather than a one-to-one basis, I finally meet Preben. I am attending a workshop and he has come along with one of the participating practitioners. Before the workshop even starts, many who are assembled are instantly attracted to the uniqueness of the energy around him. We are all touched by his gentle manner and quiet, almost reserved, demeanour. I have no idea if he possesses any real awareness or knowledge of the image he so clearly projects, but I imagine it is entirely possible he does not. His pale skin and slightly faded blond looks make him stand out and immediately identify his Scandinavian origins. Straight away, I am struck by how thin and undernourished he looks. My mothering instincts automatically come to the surface. Inwardly, I find myself smiling as I determine what he really needs is some decent food to fill him out a little. Preben is tall and rangy with not one ounce of spare flesh on his bones. His lean frame only seems to accentuate this. Around his narrow shoulders, his long, unkempt hair hangs loose and limp.

As soon as he completes his preparations, he squats down and sits cross-legged and silent in front of us. Without making eye contact with anyone, his eyelids close and he goes into his own private place and space. The deep sense of inner spiritual peace and serenity he exudes is palpable. No one doubts for a moment the presence and tranquil strength of this unassuming man.

Over the years that followed there were to be many meetings with Preben. I definitely felt a genuine bond and connection with him and his specific energy, and always looked forward enormously to our meetings. Every one of them was a testament to his unique way of leaving me wanting more. Whoever happened to be present at an event of his was richly rewarded. He would regale us with stories of time spent with the Sioux, learning all he could about their culture and the ways of the Ancestors. His knowledge was vast and he was generous in its giving. On many occasions he chose to adopt the mode of dress of his Native American brothers. That is exactly how I see him in my mind's eye, and how I choose to hold onto the memory of one very special experience.

My friend and I were looking forward to Preben coming to spend the day with us. I had made arrangements for her to pick him up at the local bus station and bring him to my home. She was concerned she might not recognise him, but I assured her that would not be a problem. It would be pretty hard to miss someone as distinctive as Preben. In that I was accurate. As soon as my friend saw the figure waiting patiently she knew who he was. Completely oblivious to the stares and curious glances of passers by, Preben stood in resplendent glory for all to see. He was certainly a sight to behold. Kitted out in buckskins and with feathers braided through his hair, he looked like a European version of a modern day warrior, minus the face painting or markings. As he crossed the doorstep of the manse in which I lived at the time, I could not help myself. The broadest grin spread across my face. Surely Preben had to have been one of the most colourful and illustrious visitors ever to enter the environs of a former Church of Scotland ministry.

What a fabulous day it turned out to be. There was an incredible energy surrounding everything we did. The hours melted away. Preben started by patiently explaining some of the history and ancient practices and customs of the Ancestors. We sat entranced. His voice was soft and reflective. He spoke with great sensitivity and understanding about the energy of Grandfather Sky reaching down to embrace us and how we in return should embrace the beautiful giving nature of Grandmother Earth as she sought to protect us and offer guidance. Preben showered us with so much incredible knowledge about Great Spirit. He showed us the ways of the four directions of the winds, and how to interpret and interact with their energies. We learnt about the power of the different moon cycles and how they could contribute and affect the outcome of our daily living. Although we had known for a long time how to cleanse and sweep auras, we were shown how to do this with sage brush and a beautiful selection of owl and eagle feathers. We were taught to acknowledge and honour every experience in life, be it good or bad. Recognising and accepting our own inner strengths and weaknesses was something we were actively encouraged to embrace.

When Preben revealed his intention to carry out the pipe ceremony my heart did a celebratory back flip. Because I had heard so much in previous visits about honouring this tradition I knew it was going to be a moment of great significance for me personally to receive such a gift from Spirit. The fact that this was so totally unexpected made the whole thing even more special.

Just as soon as Preben turned around and removed the pipe from his small backpack his whole level of energy seemed to change. If one was to try and describe what a shift in consciousness looked like then that is exactly what transpired. For a while he sat motionless, as if reacquainting himself with the pipe and its properties. It seemed to me as if every movement and action had slowed down to a snail's pace. It did not matter. This was the way Preben had chosen. He was being diligent and taking time to show us each step in the ceremonial process. I could clearly see just how precious the pipe and its ceremonial association were to him.

This was a first for my friend and me. Neither of us had ever seen a ceremonial pipe before and, excusing the pun, we were quite literally bowled over. As soon as the pipe was unwrapped from its soft cloth covering it was placed gently on the floor in front of us. The pipe was aged and remarkably plain in design. That was what made it so beautiful in my eyes. Without knowing if it was fact or not, I got a sense that the bowl of the pipe somehow represented a nurturing, feminine aspect, while the straight wooden pipe represented a strong, masculine energy. I am not sure if anyone else noticed, but I could definitely feel the energy in the room shift again. Additional elements suddenly came into play. Events sped up as powerful energies rooted and began to magnify and multiply. I opened myself up to receiving and experiencing this wonderful gift.

Preben extracted a small amount of 'K-nik K-nik', or tobacco, from the soft leather pouch hanging loosely around his neck, before packing it firmly inside the blood red stone bowl of the pipe. You could tell he was an old hand at this practice. Everything was done with such measured precision. A match was taken from a box and struck. Seconds later, the fine strands of tobacco connected with the naked flame and sprung into life. Preben lowered his head and gently blew into the bowl. With the embers glowing and the slightly sweet smell of the tobacco filling the room, Preben raised the pipe in honour of the four directions. He spoke softly in recognition of the old ways and of the Ancestors. I cannot remember exactly what the words were, but I do remember an immediate sense of connection with Spirit. Encouraged by the spoken word, a powerful, yet strangely familiar energy was activated. As the ceremony continued, my friend and I sat mesmerised. Satisfied that due honour had been paid to the directions, Preben brought the pipe to his lips and inhaled deeply. Sitting silently observing and waiting, we watched Preben's nostrils contract then expand before finally exhaling. Only after he had repeated the process for a second time was Preben ready to release the pipe from his care. Then it was our turn. We could hardly wait.

Holding the pipe in the way we had been shown it was passed first to my friend and then to me. I gave no more than a second's thought to any harm which might be incurred by filling my lungs with noxious toxins. Because I knew the inhalation effects would be temporary and minimal, I went ahead anyway. Both my friend and I repeated the short ceremony Preben had taught us. We immersed ourselves in a place of deep relaxation and companionable silence, as memories of past lives and times on the open plains intertwined and gently washed over us. To me, it felt like a spiritual coming home as the Ancestors gradually began to appear and join us around the campfires of those lives. On reflection, I have no real remembrance of how long we sat like that but my sense is it was a considerable amount of time. No matter how much I longed for a continuance, the ceremony and everything surrounding it came to its inevitable conclusion. We all offered our thanks to the Ancestors for their generosity of spirit. Although my friend and I wished the afternoon could have gone on forever, we knew in our heart of hearts that the time had come to say our farewells to the pipe.

The ceremony was just about over, but not completely. Ashes from the bowl were lovingly coaxed onto the shifting iridescent rainbow light of a large mother of pearl oyster shell. Detached from the memories it had embraced so lovingly, the pipe was wrapped up with the same care and reverence Preben had initially bestowed upon it. Bathed in the soft afterglow of ancestral connection, we sat quietly reflecting on the visitation of Spirit. It was deeply moving and such a life-enhancing experience.

To my surprise and delight, the day was not yet over. It ended with my first ever drum journey. As soon as I stepped into the experience I knew it definitely would not be my last. It was an incredible journey for my friend and me as we connected with Spirit and our power animals. We were transported to a world of our own where remembrance of self flourished. Familiar sounds of drum beat and mystical memory reached out and wrapped itself around us.

To this day I can still sense the lightest touch of delicate feathers gently brushing against my face as they smoothed and cleansed my auric senses. They felt like the softest whisper of a breath. For me, the most extraordinary part of the day was listening to the haunting sound of Preben playing his flute. While my friend and I continued our journey with Ancient Spirits the notes rose and fell and drew us into their magic. Perhaps the remarkable specialness of the whole day is responsible for the sounds lingering on in my heart. I love many different forms of music but I do not think I have ever in my entire life heard anything so profoundly moving or beautiful. Whenever my heart remembers the day my reaction is always the same. I still get goose bumps thinking about it.

Though I have not seen Preben for a long time, I do still feel inordinately blessed and privileged to have encountered him in this lifetime. I continue to regard him as a friend and someone I will be eternally grateful to for reawakening that part of my native soul. Preben is a very special person who has been blessed with many amazing gifts. The fact that he chooses to share these gifts so generously and freely with others says a great deal about the person he is. In my mind he is a rare spirit amongst men, and will always hold a special place in my heart.

new acquaintants

Every day, I make the deliberate and conscious decision to interact and work with energies. Some are constants surrounding me, whilst others are invitees. This particular aspect of my life always enthrals. At times it quite literally takes me out of myself and helps transform the ordinary into an experience of the extraordinary kind. Whether this manifests as the simplest discovery about self, or some deep-rooted anxiety being gently coaxed to the surface and finally released when I work with these powerful forces, it is always a new and thrilling experience. It never palls.

Working alongside or in conjunction with others is also exhilarating and can bring wonderful rewards. I always enjoy being around people who I know have the ability to ignite the touch paper. In the process of doing that, wheels are set in motion and memorable experiences instigated. Throughout my years of journeying, I have been lucky enough to meet one or two people who could, more often than not, be guaranteed to bring that special element of excitement combined with a sense of spiritual discovery and personal awakening to any given occasion. This next extract is about one of those persons whose energy and input always brings out the aspects of self most in need of nurture.

friendship in the making

The thing that most attracts people to Richard is the energy surrounding him. Outwardly, he appears laid back and remarkably chilled, but there is so much more to his personality than that. He exudes confidence, and his surety and quiet assertiveness in the work he carries out makes people relax and feel at ease in his presence. His humour and relaxed approach to life and spiritual journeying in general seems to inspire others. Many of those seeking guidance from the universe find themselves steered in his direction. I will always be grateful for the part Richard played in my journey.

When I set out on my own spiritual quest I was reluctant and not yet completely comfortable in my own spiritual skin. Richard, on the other hand, was already well and truly walking the path of discovery and personal reawakening. With the excesses of his rock and roll days firmly behind him, he travelled his own road towards enlightenment. He relates interesting and often amusing stories of time spent travelling in India visiting the ashrams. For every story told he has dozens of others in similar vein just waiting to be unveiled. One of his favourite stories is about the day he met Saia Baba for the first time. It turned out to be a memorable experience in more ways than one.

It was a common sight of the ashram. Hundreds of people would gather and wait patiently for Saia Baba to make an appearance. On this particular occasion, Richard was amongst those who waited. Eventually, anticipation gave way to realisation. The moment of reveal finally arrived. Surrounded by close followers, Saia Baba made his entrance. Richard watched as row upon row of devotees were blessed by the man himself. When Saia Baba reached Richard he stopped directly in front of him. Not quite knowing what to expect, Richard was completely dumbfounded when Saia Baba leaned forward and hit him on the head before moving off. Not one word was spoken in the passing.

Did this singular unexpected incident put paid to Richard returning to India? Not one bit. He visited the ashram again over the years. There was, however, no repeat of his unique experience with Saia Baba.

Responsibility for setting up the first ever Reiki centre in Scotland is partly down to Richard. Reluctant to be just talking the talk, he definitely had the courage to walk his walk. In doing so he paved the path for others to follow. In all the time I have known him he has consistently proven himself a wonderful catalyst to a huge array of souls struggling to find their way in life. Countless persons seek his counsel. Many take on board his advice. He is good at listening and will always try and be truthful with people, whist encouraging them to see their own truth. It is pretty much the case of what you see is what you get with Richard. A lot of people like to believe they know him well and understand him. For all his showmanship and apparent transparency, at times the reality is there is a side to him that he chooses to share with only a few. He can be disarmingly complex. A larger than life character, he explodes into people's lives and completely bowls them over. I am so glad I got to know him and we have become friends. Whenever I think of him I always want to smile.

changing times

Although I have a treasure chest of memories, sitting down and writing about Richard and any spiritual experiences we shared is actually a great deal harder to do than I imagined. I suppose in order for me to set the wheels in motion and share part of my recollections, it is probably best if I start at the very beginning.

The first time Richard's name was mentioned in conversation I must admit I had never heard of him. This was hardly surprising. I was just starting my foray into all things otherworldly and had no idea of the already established names on the spiritual, or what some chose to refer to then as the 'new age' scene. All my energy had, up to that point, been focused on taking the first tentative footsteps on a journey of reawakening and self-discovery. From my novel and somewhat idealistic viewpoint, the road ahead appeared so straight and easily traversable. It promised so much. I had the belief that the path I walked upon, and the route I was taking, would in time grant me access towards my own personal spiritual growth and enlightenment. Those were the thoughts uppermost in my mind and holding my attention. Richard had not yet popped up on my radar screen.

I knew changes to the way I lived my life were definitely on the way. What information I had gleaned on the Laws of Attraction and their direct relationship to me proved scant, but remarkably accurate. The Laws had not just been dawdling in the slow lane of life and living. Somewhere along the way, The Laws had picked up speed and gone into overdrive. As a result, a sense and consciousness built up around that and the world sat up and paid attention. The Laws had been well and truly activated.

This did not mean to say things were straightforward. Sensing the subtle shift in consciousness was completely different to trying to live in, and from, that conscious place. People in general still had an air of the restless spirit about them. They looked for answers to questions they could give no clear definition to. Many felt genuinely disenchanted with their lives. Battles raged deep within as resolution was sought. Surely there had to be more to life and the way it was being lived?

So, the beginnings of a groundswell reflecting this disenchantment started to gain momentum. The number of people directly crossing my pathway increased. It was a relief knowing I was not alone in my thinking or my questioning. Almost everyone I met at that time appeared to be in search of an elusive something they felt was missing from their lives. If only this something could be found, perhaps it would act as a magical panacea to the greatest conundrum of all, and that was the meaning of life itself. Once provenance of this something was in their possession, somehow lives would be transformed forever, and any sense of abandonment people might have experienced would be reversed.

Becoming whole was what people appeared to be longing for. At times, it all seemed so tantalisingly close. Many felt sure instant gratification was well within their grasp. They naively clung to the belief that somehow their lives would be immediately transformed. The missing piece of the puzzle would fall into place and they would then feel complete in every way. Although people did not realise it at the time, the logic behind their thinking was impaired. Probably because none of us knew any better, we pursued this so called something for years before realising our folly. Some I know are still searching to this day.

It was an exciting time exploring all the avenues offering a meaning to life. I greeted each and every one of these new encounters and introductions with an air of great expectancy and anticipation. New things happening meant new opportunities arising, and I was all for that. It also meant new people would be coming into my life.

so to the man himself

When I laid eyes on Richard for the very first time he was peering over a banister three floors above me. Almost straight away I realised I would have to call on his services. I needed help and it was not of a spiritual nature. No matter how much I tried to position my body there was no way at all for me to climb the impossibly narrow staircase and join both him and the group which had assembled upstairs. In a few short strides, my predicament was resolved. Richard came bounding down the stairs to the rescue. He made what took place next seem so effortless. With little or no assistance he gallantly carried out a fireman's lift manoeuvre. Placing one foot firmly in front of the other he proceeded to carry me up the three flights of vertiginous stairs. Whilst he may very well have been feeling assured, I, on the other hand, was not. Holding on for grim life, I closed my eyes and nervously whispered words of encouragement to a silent God.

It was not the most auspicious start to the day, nor was it the way in which I normally go about getting to know someone. It did, however, get me where I needed to be in order to participate. So, a day of magic for me, and dramatic experiences and spiritual encounters for others, slowly began to unravel. Although neither of us realised it at the time, a lengthy friendship with Richard had just been kick-started.

I soon discovered a workshop was not a workshop without the name Richard being brought up by someone. He had a large following, both at home and abroad, and was immensely charismatic and entertaining. An accomplished raconteur, he could certainly tell a story or two about his own spiritual quest and the interesting characters he had met along the way. He had a presence about him that few could rival. Whenever word got out that Richard was about to do one of his weekend workshops, there was never a shortage of people rushing to sign up for the event. It did not seem to bother anyone that the subject matter was seldom, if ever, clearly stated in advance. Everyone had an understanding that amazing 'things' would happen over the period of those two days. No topic or subject was considered off limits or out of bounds. The crazier and more bizarre the events, the more people seemed to enjoy it. His experience in working with energies meant he was always in demand. People could not seem to get enough of him.

I can still remember those early years and the workshops. Very few practitioners of energy work had the ability to excite people the way

Richard did. Along with the serious stuff that presented itself, there was always room left over for laughter and fun. Looking back reminds me just how crazy those times actually were. Entire weekends were given over to the ascension process and spiritual exploration. If we found ourselves directed towards energies stuck between earthly and other realms, we would assist in moving those energies towards the Light. Sometimes, Richard would bring out Tarot cards and do readings for people. Other occasions might be spent discussing divination or numerology or past life experiences. The deeper we travelled on our inner journeys, the more rewarding the outcome. Someone I know very well would quite regularly feel herself shape-shifting. Rising on the air currents, she would become one with an eagle flying over the Grand Canyon. When she was not being an eagle, she occasionally sensed herself in leonine form. It was all good sustenance for hungry initiates. Psychic surgery was for several years a particular favourite for many, and when it came to removing entities, Richard was the one person you wanted by your side. He had a very unique and distinctive style. Occasionally, he would sit cross-legged like some ancient guru or wise man and practice what is often commonly referred to as healing. When he had no particular indication of what to do next, he would just sit in silence waiting for guidance or divine inspiration.

I found the workshops with direct input from the angelic realms intriguing for several reasons. Richard rarely called upon angels for assistance. Occasionally, he might seek guidance and make a request to Archangel Michael for protection. I suspect that was more of a security thing for the benefit of the group than any deep relationship he might acknowledge having with Archangel Michael. It always struck me as unusual that Richard had little or no real interest in connecting with angelic energies. Whilst respectful of others spiritual experiences, he could at times seem detached somehow from those choosing to go down the angelic route. I am not sure if he still feels that way. Perhaps the intervening years have opened him up to more celestial experiences. Perhaps they have not. Whatever the case may or may not be, the universe will have gifted Richard with exactly what is right for him.

The moment Richard placed his beautiful carved figure of Horus directly in front of us everyone in the room would sense a subtle shift in energy. Horus generally equated to ancient mystical energies being channelled. That always generated a definite frisson of additional excitement and expectation. Would it be a day for the ancient Egyptian energies of Isis and Horus to surface, or would we reconnect with the

Ancestors of the Thunder or Cloud people again? Sun Cloud was an energy which had a particular attachment to Richard and he would often come through. The thing with channelling was none of us could really predict who or what might decide to make its presence known, or the words that were likely to be imparted.

In those early days I was always extremely cautious when it came to any form of channelling. Over the years, however, confidence in my own abilities expressed itself. As a result, I became more comfortable with the energies invoked through direct channelling. If asked today I would always advise people to take care when they are doing ANY form of energy work. When it comes to channelling I would advise everyone to be particularly careful. I know a lot of people who have found themselves in difficult straights because they did not take adequate precaution and follow a few basic principles when channelling. Powerful elements are at work during channelling and it is very easy for energies which are not of the Light to filter through. So many people today talk about channelling being easy. Anyone who wishes can do it. It is not so very difficult, is it? Because some people channel safely and successfully, others presume they can automatically channel for themselves. It is exactly because people hold this naive view that channelling in inexperienced hands can so often be unpredictable and challenging. It happens more often than people realise. What seems initially like an innocent enough experiment ends up being a bad experience. If you do not know what you are doing it can be extremely unsafe, so please do not venture to invite energies of which you have no knowing or understanding.

Richard would occasionally bring along another favourite item of his. It was a large labradorite sphere and he would always place it right by his side. All we could do was imagine just what magic lay in the impenetrable depths of this particular stone. Richard was always cautious and a little reluctant to let anyone touch either Horus or the sphere. When I learnt recently from him that he had given both Horus and the sphere away a long time ago I was surprised. He had such a strong attachment to them. I suppose that is the thing about forming an attachment with iconic material objects. Times change and so do we. The desire to hold onto such things is no longer necessary or relevant to our lives.

Thinking again about those early workshops, I remember everyone took channelling and extending the boundaries and parameters of understanding in their stride. It all felt perfectly normal for the times we were living in. As we safely opened ourselves up to new experiences, nothing was too fantastical for our absorbing, inquiring minds. Occasionally, negative energies or forces would come into play. The universe looked out for us and we were given instruction on how to deal with any given situation. As a result, we learnt from our experiences and moved forward again.

stranger in the midst

It had been a few months since I had last seen Richard. Here he was again, about to do a weekend workshop. Both he and a friend of mine from the west were staying over. I cannot remember the topic of the workshop, but I have memory of the morning session having gone well. As soon as the afternoon session got under way, many in our group started to sense a heavy energy building up around us. It seemed to be shrouded in an impenetrable mist, and emitted a sense of deep mourning. This aspect of the energy acted like a powerful magnet drawing us ever closer to its main source. A message filtered through the expectant consciousness. Something somewhere was signalling its distress and, whether we wanted to or not, we were being guided straight towards it. As soon as we picked up on that cry for help we tuned directly into it. Though no one voiced it, there was an understanding that ancient energies somewhere were calling out for assistance. With only a few exceptions, I would say that almost everyone in the room that day felt the power of the forces at work. Out of nowhere, an air of immediacy sprung up. It was so close you could reach out and touch it. There was an unexpressed expectation that our help was needed, but we lacked clear direction and did not know what form that help would take. The more we tried to understand what was required of us, the more complicated everything seemed to become. Rallying to the cry for help was not going to be as straightforward as we imagined. It was impossible to think with any degree of clarity or conviction. Our judgement felt as clouded as the energy itself.

Without too much probing on the part of the group, one aspect of the whole proceedings did eventually make itself known to us. It involved an ancestral feminine energy. Completely bogged down, the energy was struggling to disengage and distance itself from the ancient ties and forces that bound it. Armed with this knowledge, our group felt sure we could move forward and help the embattled energy. We were wrong. As it turned out, we were going to need something further than the information currently on offer. All we could do at that point was continue to seek guidance on what to do next. What was it about this specific energy/entity that made it differ from previous encounters we had experienced? Why were we not able to see what needed to be seen? The timing of what happened next could not have been bettered. I remember having what is referred to as a 'light bulb moment'. Although the moment was anything but light or bright, it was nonetheless revealing. Suddenly, several quite disturbing images of contorted skeletons laying beneath heavily impacted ground began seeping through my consciousness.

It was relatively easy identifying the roughly hewn ground and irregular markings of the elongated burial plots. What surprised me more than anything else was the fact I knew the exact location of the grave site. I also had knowledge, if not an understanding, that instead of the customary practice of one body in a coffin, two bodies had been placed in each coffin for burial. Intuition told me what we faced that day definitely had something to do with those burials. Though I was sure that somewhere in the recesses of memory there was a reason why this particular practice was carried out, I could not quite grasp the memory and had to let it go.

When I relayed my experience to the group everyone seemed relieved. Finally, we had something to work with and tune into. By uniting as one and declaring our positive intentions we could direct our focus of attention and resolve the situation.

Just as the intention was about to be set, several of us quite literally felt ourselves being physically pulled in a different direction. We left the sacred space of the room we were in, crossed over the wide hallway and followed our intuition straight through to the kitchen at the side of the house. Immediately, the energy in the room intensified. As it wrapped itself firmly around me, I somehow had a sense of almost forcefully being contained and restrained in that one space. It wasn't a negative thing and I felt comfortable with it.

A dramatic and dynamic shift had definitely taken place. We all felt it. When a giant vortex of spiralling energy opened up the sensation was instantaneous. We could feel ourselves being picked up and sucked deeper and deeper towards its centre. Something else was happening, over and above that. Again, for me, it was an intuitive thing. Through all the confusion, I sensed the imminent arrival of important information. Blocking out everything else going on around me, I concentrated hard on being the recipient of that information. It did not disappoint in its delivery or content.

My memory was triggered into remembrances of a medieval burial site. Running parallel to the ley lines on which my house stood, it lay a short distance away at the furthermost boundary of the seasonal ploughed fields in the north east section of the village. Skirting the edges of a dry stone dyke, the site jutted out and straddled the wild, gorse-infused grasses overlooking the rugged coastline. Pilgrims of old used to walk along the coastal path en route to St Andrews. No gravestones marked the site, so I would not have imagined for one minute that many people knew of the existence of the graves.

Once the group became aware of the connection between the graves and the energy seeking help, everything seemed to quickly fall into place. Knowing the trapped energy was singular and feminine helped create an image in everyone's minds. We wasted no more time and quickly refocused and set to work. Using the powers we had been blessed with helped the group bring resolution to the plight of the moribund energy. Shifting something so deeply entrenched took far longer to achieve than most of us imagined it would, but eventually the troubled spirit was released and made its way towards the Light. No longer able to control or hold onto a waning power, the centuries old stranglehold finally gave up the fight and, as a result, was relegated to memory. Everyone knew the exact moment the gap between any remaining essence of the deceased and the Divine was bridged. We could all feel the gracious transition towards the Light and were thankful. Balance and Light had been restored once again.

People were reluctant to leave after the workshop. Keen to chat to Richard and talk over the events of the day, some had lingered longer than normal. As a result our evening meal was delayed by a good couple of hours. By the time we eventually got around to eating we were ravenous and made short work of the food on offer. Relaxing afterwards in the kitchen, the three of us sat in reflective mood, quietly drinking coffee. As we talked, we wondered what the following day might bring. Would it be as interesting and challenging as today had been, or would it be a gentler affair?

I had been thinking I might just leave Richard and my friend to their own devices and take myself off to bed when the front door bell rang. My eyes automatically went to the hands on the old kitchen clock. It was just after half past ten. Who could be calling so late in the evening? I wondered. My initial reaction was to presume that something must be wrong, or somebody was in need of help. No one in their right mind would choose to be out and about on such a miserable night. A storm was raging outside and the rain had not let up for one single minute. I was glad the three of us were all safe inside.

Moving out into the hall, I switched on the outside lights. The whole front of the house immediately lit up. Through the vestibule window I could just make out the head and shoulders of a figure. At that point I could not determine whether the figure was male or female. Facing away and hunched right up against the arched stone overhang of the doorway, the figure was trying its level best to shelter from the rain. Most of the lights in the house were now on but the figure made no attempt to turn his or her face towards the lights. My initial instinct was to hurry and get the figure out of the rain and into the warm environs of the house. No sooner had the thought registered than I found myself questioning it. What had seemed so clear cut only seconds previously suddenly took on a different perspective, and I found myself begin to waver a little. For some unknown reason, I began to feel a certain reluctance to answer the door. Some inner sense kicked in and the first tiny twinges of unease took hold and toyed with my thought process. When my own intuition sent up the first red flag of warning I knew something untoward was happening and I must be cautious. Whatever the reason behind it all, some indefinable thing about the figure made me feel uncomfortable. Without understanding why, I felt hairs rise at the back of my neck. It was all a little odd. Who was this figure and why the nocturnal appearance? What was it about the late night visitor that had started to actively gnaw away at my normally fluid decision making? Why did I suddenly feel so riddled with uncertainty? As questions began lining up back-to-back, I did not know quite what to make of it.

Amidst the state of mind confusion, I was certain of one thing. Finding my house in the pitch dark would have been a bit of a challenge for anyone. It was difficult to imagine someone randomly happening across it by chance. There were no street lights or illuminated signposts to guide anyone. Up an old, unlit farm track and some distance from all the other properties in the village, the house was not the most accessible property in the neighbourhood. It certainly could not be seen easily from the main road, nor would one just stumble upon it. I surmised the figure seeking protection from the ravages of the storm definitely had to have known the location of my house.

I found myself in a bit of a quandary. Time gave the sense of lapsing into an indeterminable vacuum. In fact, it took only seconds for me to process all these random, runaway thoughts. What I really needed to know was should I listen to what my gut instinct was telling me or not? Should I go against all the safety guidelines I had put in place for myself? While those specific questions remained unanswered, I had the presence of mind to place additional protection around myself. Why, you may ask, did I do that? The answer is I felt an overwhelming need to do so.

It was a really strange thing and something that even today I find difficult to put into words. The figure was still standing outside my house. On the inside, I felt my perception of what was real and what was not suddenly shift. In the time it took me to blink, the balance in the energy surrounding me altered. It came as a bit of a shock when I was faced with the knowledge that I no longer had full control over what was about to transpire. Some other element/energy had entered the equation and was now orchestrating and directing events.

What happened next was bizarre. Without knowing why exactly, I intuitively sensed the figure had begun to play some form of psychological mind game with me. At the time it was impossible to know the content or parameters of the game. Stranger still was the sensation I had of a gauntlet being thrown down and a direct challenge made. Instinct and inner knowing told me I was about to be tested in some way. Whatever I chose to do in the next few minutes would determine the final outcome of this strange encounter. Would I rise to the challenge and pick up the gauntlet?

Even as I write this, I can understand how improbable all of this sounds, but I cannot explain it any other way. Everything happened exactly as I have described it. Of course, I was aware of unique elements at work, yet I did not feel in the least bit fearful. The figure had neither said nor done anything which would warrant me seeing and viewing events in such a way. The conclusions I had reached were of my own making. I did sense everything was exactly the way it should be.

It did not take any time at all for me to recognise the figure's ability to manifest a particularly powerful energy. At one point I even got the ridiculous notion the figure was almost defying me to open the door and acknowledge its presence. All this craziness was bouncing around in my head, complicating any rational thought. For my own sanity and equilibrium I really had to try and restore some sort of balance. Firstly, I could make a start by asking myself if I actually wanted the figure to enter my house or not?

When it came right down to it there was never any question about what I would do next. Never in my life had I turned anyone away from my door. If some game or divine challenge was in the process of being enacted I was certainly up for it.

I have no idea what emotions the figure experienced when I turned the handle and opened the door. She did seem a little surprised when, instead of keeping her standing on the doorstep, I asked her to step inside. I marvelled at just how quickly my thought process had turned around and given ground. Not only did I ask her in, it was now vital to me that she actually accept my invitation and come inside. I had an awareness and understanding that I must play my part by engaging her in dialogue. Until this was possible, everything would remain the mystery it was.

Everything took on the air of the surreal. I had an inherent sense of some otherworldly thing going on, yet could not have said with any degree of confidence what that thing was. The young woman was a pitiful looking sight. Her complexion had a waxy, almost opaque transparency. I could tell from her general demeanour she was completely exhausted. She appeared to struggle a little with my invitation. Eventually, she stepped inside out of the rain. Without suitable outer garments to protect her against the elements, her clothing was soaked through. This only seemed to further accentuate her frailty. I felt a tremendous swell of compassion for my bedraggled visitor. My heart rose and went out to her. She seemed to sense this and made her first positive eye contact with me. I quickly established that beneath the earthly mask lay another identity. Perhaps I should have been a little shocked and taken aback. As much as this newfound reality existed, I was not in the least bit shocked. If truth be told, I was probably half expecting the revelation. The moment I acknowledged the connection as credible, some unspoken understanding passed between us. I smiled encouragingly at her. She looked down at her feet. Not one word crossed her lips.

I thought the evening could not get any stranger, yet it did. Undaunted, and determined to find out at least something of my guest, I proceeded to ask if I could be of assistance. There then followed a most bizarre conversation.

Although the young woman never revealed her name, I quickly established she was American. Ill equipped for night walking, she had come to my house seeking to identify the location of a stone wall somewhere in the village where I lived. At first I did not know if I had heard her correctly, but with a little more probing, soon determined that I had. In order to discover just what direction the story would end up taking us both, I decided to go along with it. Had she been to any other houses to make enquiries I asked? She said she had not. The wall had apparently been written about by the poet Robert Frost.

Did I know the poet she inquired? I did. With little more to go on than a solitary line part way through a poem, and no indication of where the wall might be, she had travelled from the United States to Scotland hoping to find the aforementioned wall. Her sole objective was to visit the site in the poem. In the maelstrom of confusion in my head one single, silly, superfluous thought emerged and rose to the surface. How on earth did she hope to find the wall in the pitch dark without a torch or clear direction?

She said she was a student attending a local university. My natural reaction was to presume she was attending St. Andrews University a few miles away. I was glad therefore to have some common ground at last on which to build a conversation. In that presumption, I was entirely mistaken. I do not think she was expecting or indeed wishing any protracted dialogue. Interacting with others was normally relatively straightforward for me. What few words we were exchanging began to feel laboured and awkward. Within minutes of the conversation starting, it almost ground to a halt. Why, I asked myself for the umpteenth time, had this particular young woman turned up on my doorstep? Did she honestly expect me to believe her story about the wall? What did she really want from me? If indeed one existed, what was her true agenda that night?

Perhaps it was the frustration of my inability to give her the information she sought, but I could definitely sense her agitation. It was palpable. What was she trying to get across to me and why was I causing her to feel so agitated? I felt myself out of my depth and beginning to flounder a little. Why? I asked myself. What was it I was failing to understand? Other than continuing to try and help her, I did not know what else I could do.

There was a message hidden somewhere within everything which was taking place. What was it? The young woman continued to be agitated. I sensed her state of confusion increase and tried to get the message across that I was there to help her. When I asked her about her studies she could not remember what subject she was studying, or where she was supposed to be studying. She had no recollection at all of where she was living. This whole thing was getting stranger by the minute. When I heard her blurt out that she had no place to stay and would spend the night out in the open I really began to feel concerned. 'Nobody' I said to myself 'should be sleeping rough on such a dreadful night'. It was at that moment I remembered who and what I was dealing with. This was all new and slightly uncharted territory for me. What on earth was I supposed to do now? In other circumstances

I would not have thought twice about offering to put someone up, but I recognised how absurd the notion actually was. There was nothing normal about these circumstances. So, where did I go from here?

Sensing we had reached a bit of an impasse, I tried picking up where we had left off. Although very little of what she said made any sense at all to me, the woman continued to press for information about the wall. Was I certain I did not know where the wall was? I could sense her reluctance to let go of the matter. It felt to me as if this one tenuous thread and point of reference was the only thing holding everything together.

On reflection, of course it was a lot easier to recognise things were not as they seemed, and that some other thing lay beneath the guise of supposed reality being enacted. Because everything was happening so quickly, I did not have the luxury of time to immediately pick up on that aspect. As I continued to struggle to take the whole thing forward, Richard and my friend chose that particular moment to join the young woman and me in the hallway. The figure did notice them, but said nothing by way of recognition or inclusion. As she continued to look at me, I sensed the energy which bound the two of us begin to shift and dissipate. I became acutely conscious of a delicate balance between urgency to help and time somehow about to run out. Richard and my friend stood quietly taking in what they could of the situation. Their silence seemed to say everything.

The four of us remained in the hallway for several minutes more. Whatever the true reasons for the visit of the young woman, I knew I wanted to continue offering assistance. If it was within my power to give her definitive answers, I would have. Perhaps I just had not known the correct questions to ask her. As a result of this, she had not been able to guide me towards finding resolution to her questioning. It was so frustrating, suddenly feeling everything beginning to slip away from me.

In the end, she was the one who called a halt to proceedings. Her late night visitation drew to a close. I did not know if I was happy or sad that our strange encounter had reached its conclusion. Instead of feeling positive, I was left with a feeling of failing to complete something so fundamental it would have repercussions and affect the young woman forever. I instinctively knew she had been badly let down by my inability to fully comprehend and interpret what was expected of me.

The young woman was gracious in her thanks. As she began to step away, she appeared weighted down with a deep sadness. With one final haunting look she turned away from the safe shelter of my home and disappeared into the dark, stormy night.

To say I was confused was a bit of an understatement. What I really needed was the quiet, safe sanctuary of my bedroom. I knew I had to be alone with my thoughts. Any further conversation with Richard and my friend was a distraction I could well do without. I needed time to think about what had just taken place. Making my excuses was easy and caused no offence. I headed straight upstairs towards the small library. In the poetry section I found the book I was looking for.

Safely ensconced in my bed, I picked up the old worn copy of works by Robert Frost. Perhaps it was luck, or even some divine intervention, which guided me immediately to the page. There in black and white on the faded curled pages was a poem which made reference to a stone wall in the village in which I lived. It was, of course, the stone wall the young woman sought. As I read the poem I felt the goose bumps rise. Straight away, I recognised the location of the wall. It marked the boundary between field and sea and lay adjacent to the ancient burial site.

As I lay in bed trying to make sense of it all, thoughts bombarded me from every direction. I could not shake the image of the young woman from my mind. What I could not understand was the lingering sense of urgency which still existed. The more I thought about it, the more I realised that the events of the afternoon and the late night visit by the young woman were related. I asked myself over and over again what the young woman needed from me. Why had I been so blind and not recognised what I was supposed to do?

When the penny finally dropped of course everything became as clear as the clearest crystal waters. I was right in my knowing that the young woman needed something very specific that night. With few options open to her, she had reacted to events as they unfolded in the only way she knew how. As another lost soul desperately seeking a way to the Light, she had, by a somewhat circuitous route, introduced herself into the reality that represented my life. Attracted to the energy and Light surrounding the events of the afternoon, she had been guided to me and my home. Like the soul that had been helped towards the Light, she also needed to move on towards the Light. Once I became aware of this I was able to gradually pick up the threads of connecting with her soul essence. It was not essential for me to know anything about the history of the young woman. My job was to assist her in any way I could.

I wasted no time in calling for assistance. It came within an instant. Light from everything which is Light flooded the consciousness of every living cell of every living thing. Celestial and Divine energies were gentle as they wrapped themselves around the figure. Entrusting herself over to their care, the final remaining aspect of the figure rose and made her way towards the Light.

In a day full of extraordinary moments this perhaps was the most extraordinary for me. I felt my heartbeat quicken then expand. From Heaven's cathedral a choir full of angels burst into exquisite, harmonious song. My mysterious visitor was finally guided home to the Light. Her long, lonely struggle to be free from earthly dominion was over.

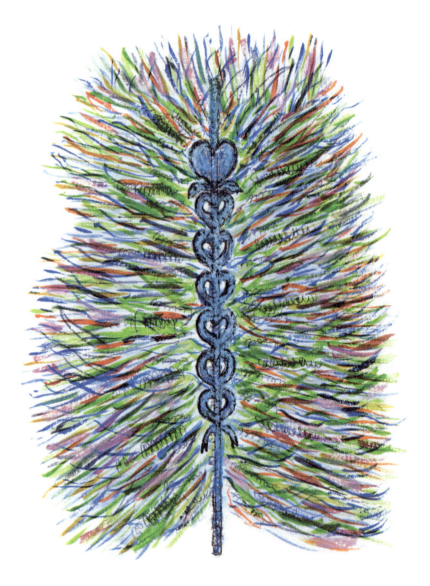

Extract no. 4:
The Isis + Hathor blessing staff

This Staff came into my life almost one year ago, in the summer of 2003. It was the last of four extraordinary energy Staffs to be gifted to me by Spirit. From the outset, I knew that this particular Staff would test me on so many more levels than the previous three. I had never encountered anything quite like it in my life before. Nothing about this unique Staff, or the clear interaction between the energy and the Staff, could have prepared me for the impact of experiencing, for the very first time, the full extent of the energy emanating from the Staff. It was astonishing. I was desperate to learn all I could about the Staff and its true potential.

Although I did not immediately understand the precise power and exact workings of the Staff, it did not take any time at all for me to acknowledge it would become a benchmark for much of my future work. In that prediction I was accurate. Trying to understand the Staff and decipher its message was, however, a wholly different prospect and proved to be both complex and thoroughly challenging. Initially, it was almost impossible for me to predict just how I would be able to incorporate the Staff into my life. It was certainly one of the most difficult energies to interpret and put to proper usage.

Out of all my experiences and workings with some truly amazing forms of energy, what I write about next is perhaps the most memorable.

the sound healing

I had already been on my spiritual quest for quite some time. Whilst I would not say I had fully fledged from the nest, at that particular juncture I was not so very far from doing so. As I navigated and steered a hesitant course through my voyage of self discovery, familiar aspects of previous spiritual adventures rose up to greet me along the way. I had opportunities to explore exciting new concepts of reality and extend my own boundaries of understanding. Weird and wonderful things happened. I have never been one to just accept weird as necessarily being good, or the right thing for me. As tempting as the prospect of an otherworldly experience might have been, I had always been guided to go with my gut instinct. Intuitively, everything had to feel right. Just because something presented itself to me, it did not automatically follow that that something should go unchallenged. Only when I was as satisfied as I could be did I open myself fully to the experience. I determined that so long as these experiences were for my highest good, and came directly from Source, then I would welcome them and embrace those opportunities with open arms.

The walled garden beckoned, enticing us with promises of shelter. It was not enough of a temptation. Instead of going outside, my friend and I made the decision to sit beside the old, but perfectly functional Rayburn in the kitchen. It was such a grey, windy day and we wanted to banish the chills and embrace the warmth. With our own sense of ceremony, we created sacred space in preparation of the afternoon ahead. We settled down and invited the appropriate energies of the day to grace us with their presence. Our intentions for a safe and favourable outcome had been set. I knew the moment we invoked the energies we would not have long to wait. Within seconds of the invitation being proffered, it became obvious events would unfold at a faster than usual pace. From the outset, I instantly got the sense that the sound healing I was about to receive from my friend would be unlike past experiences of working with sound. I succumbed and allowed the energies to work their magic on me. Having a foot in more than one world was about to reward me with something truly exceptional.

Within seconds, I found myself being both forcefully and physically transported through time. This was not a new experience for me. In the past, I had had numerous similar encounters. Travelling through space and time always felt like the most natural thing in the world to me. Because I was comfortable with the whole process, it held no real fear for me. This time would prove to be no different.

The space I was transported to was familiar. Intuitively, I recognised this as a chamber inside one of the Pyramids, though which I could not say. The chamber was immense. Through lack of trespass, the floor had formed a deep, crisp outer layer over the finer grains of sandstone. The crispness reminded me of wintertime back home after the first heavy snowfalls. With no virgin footprints to leave their mark, the weight of the snow would cause the ground to become compacted and rigidly pristine. The floor of the chamber looked remarkably untrammelled. Given its history, and the fact the chamber was in all probability still sealed after the demise of a pharaoh millennia ago, this was no great surprise. I longed to breathe in deeply and catch my breath, but the air was thick and heavy, and smelt noxious. There did not appear to be any apparent light source, yet somehow there was light. Surprisingly, even though the visibility within the chamber was extensively compromised, there was enough for me to still see. If I closed my eyes just a fraction of the way, my line of vision would not become too impeded.

The impression of stillness before something monumental about to take place lasted only a fraction of a second. A chilling wind sprung up from nowhere, whipping particles of sand-like substance around my entire body. I could feel my legs stinging and nipping as the sand bruised my skin. In that slightly blinkered moment, the chamber came alive and reverberated with the sound of the unrelenting wind and a ferocious energy being unleashed.

My vision finally cleared enough, and I was able to gain some additional perspective of my surroundings. I was left feeling completely insignificant to the situation I found myself inhabiting. As I began to try and focus, I noticed tall Beings of Light in long, loose-flowing robes of finely woven, cream coloured fabric observing me from the sides of the chamber. All looked identical and quite inseparable. There were no significant marks or defining features to help distinguish one from the other. They stared straight ahead like inscrutable, unfathomable sentinels from my long and distant past. I had a knowing that we shared memories, yet what those memories were I could not recall. The Beings stood shoulder-to-shoulder, lining every single perimeter inch of the chamber. My eyes scanned the chamber, trying to absorb their essence. The impracticality of that became all too apparent when I realised there must have been several hundred of them. Memories of other mighty Beings of Light called the Sirian Surgeons were immediately rekindled. They had, in the past, been inordinately generous in sharing their energies with me. I knew I was not alone. When invited to do so, they would gift and restore many with their extraordinary healing abilities. Although there were similarities, the Beings in front of me projected an entirely different form of energy. I automatically knew that they were the guardians and sole protectors of the chamber. They had inherited all the secrets and mysteries in the chamber's long, eventful history. So long as I remained within the chamber, they would also protect and guard me.

In a strange contradiction, these amazing guardian Beings stood silently, yet knowingly, mouthing ancient dialects in a slow, rhythmical beat. I heard their silent words and understood their meaning. By accepting the knowledge, I allowed the words to become a part of my consciousness. It was a strangely familiar sensation to find myself becoming the recipient of ancient information. I thanked the Beings for the honour they were bestowing upon me.

There was no real time to give the concept of fear so much as one single solitary ounce of recognition or acknowledgement. I was too busy concentrating on trying to remain upright. The force and the intensity of the wind threatened to overpower me. Thankfully, the struggle was short lived. In no time at all the same wind, which had tried so hard to unbalance and dislodge my precarious foothold, was pushed to the outermost extremities of my mind. Instantly, I became preoccupied with something far more pressing. My mind was alerted to a new development unfolding. I knew something else was beginning to happen deep beneath the bowels of the Pyramid. What I had no clear understanding of just then was how this something would turn out to be so powerful, and hold more knowledge than anything I had previously encountered.

I sensed the movement a fraction of a second before I actually felt it. Suddenly, the ground underneath my feet began to fracture. Some phenomenal force was at work. Deep, irregular chasms appeared. I began to get a sense of being in the middle of some bizarre sequence from a fantasy fiction film. What happened next only added to my confusion. From the central part of what remained of the chamber floor, two powerful whirling columns rose up separately just in front of me. A sense of my own vulnerability rose along with them. I saw the columns expand and stretch upwards. Their dimensions dwarfed me. As I watched, I could see particles from the columns rapidly peel away and detach themselves. The columns appeared to vaporise somehow. Instantly, they took on the shape of two impossibly oversized cobras. They parried and writhed like duelling contortionists. Each sought to rise above the other in some habitual, ritualistic frenzy. I looked on in astonishment and mute fascination as the snakes continued to twist around each other. I blinked, and in that blinking everything changed. No trace of the once magnificent regal cobras remained. They had disappeared. Slowly, a more solid structure began to emerge. There was no phoenix rising from any ashes, but the impact was no less profound. A Staff, reminiscent of a cross between the Caduceus symbol and the DNA symbol, was miraculously created before my very eyes.

Hands appeared as if from nowhere and presented me with the Staff. I reached forward, as though it was the most natural thing in the world to be doing so. As soon as I held the Staff, I immediately got a real sense of its divine energy. The Staff was spectacular. Its beauty and power astounded me. It pulsated and vibrated with an energy the likes of which I had never seen before. Every single colour in the entire known spectrum seemed to snake out from the central column of the Staff. Those colours were pure energy. I could look at nothing else. I could see nothing else. The colours and energies gently wrapped around me. My mind was immersed in, and suffused by, the sheer wonder of it all. I could feel the colours wash over me and become a part of me and my otherworld consciousness. I can remember thinking that, even if it was only for a few short minutes, all I really wanted at that moment was for time to stand completely still. I needed to experience and have at least some inkling or understanding of this incredible thing which was being gifted to me. That did not happen.

There was no time in the real sense to even register whether the hands that presented me with the Staff were male or female. I think I was inclined to veer towards the feminine, but I was not entirely convinced. That moment of presentation was an extraordinarily powerful one, and one which left me feeling enormously empowered. My mind was racing. How had events conspired to bring this all together? Why now? Why me? What was so special about me that I should be chosen as the recipient of such a gift? I had no answers, not back then anyway, to any of my questions.

My emotions started to surface and interfere with what little discernible thought yet remained. I could feel my heart rate quicken and tear ducts swell in recognition. Regaining control of those runaway emotions turned out to be a difficult process. It would have been so easy at that point to become completely overwhelmed by the events and call a halt to proceedings. I knew I did not want an ending to my experience. What I really sought was a continuance of that experience. If I had any chance at all of achieving that, I would have to find extra resources from deep within my energy bank. I wasted no time in stating my intention to hold onto that thought. Some other greater power must have been in agreement with me, for it gave me the wisdom and the strength to hold fast and keep my experience moving in a forward direction.

The wind inside the chamber was no longer on a collision course with me and my senses. It calmed down and granted me the peace I so desperately craved. The brilliance and constant flow of energy from the Staff had immediate effect. It forced the light in the chamber to alter again. Along with that came other dramatic changes. Instantly, I got the sense of arms reaching out to embrace and support me. It was a wonderfully comforting sensation. I realised almost straight away that this was more than a case of simply being supported. I knew, instinctively, that I was being honoured and blessed.

One by one, ancient and venerated Goddesses and Priestesses and other Luminous Celestial Beings entered the periphery of my line of vision. They trod softly and glided slowly towards me, until they stood in a wide semi-circle before me. In their hands they carried long grasses and papyrus reeds. Many bore the same delicate apricot colouring of other Beings I had encountered in previous visitations. The majority of the Goddesses and their energies were, however, unknown to me. I did not know whom I should turn my gaze upon first.

Gigantic sacred geometrical symbols began to take form. At first, the movement was slow, almost halting. Gradually, the symbols took on a life of their own and began to float around me. They had a fluidity about them which drew me towards their energy, tempting me with their proximity. I tried assimilating and making sense of the spellbinding rainbow-hued symbols. I cannot imagine why I even toyed with the idea. It was completely unrealistic and a physical impossibility. The longing I had to reach out and somehow wrap my fingers around those shapes was nonetheless very powerful and hard to resist. Round and around the symbols went. It was almost as though they were teasing me with the promise of all the knowledge and wisdom of the universe. Still, the sacred symbols circled and spun their geometric wizardry around me. It was mesmeric and made me think of a synchronised balletic performance.

So many diverse energies were coming together within the chamber. They were far too numerous to count, and all were vying for space and recognition inside my head. If the energies had been of a singular nature, I might have had a better understanding of their properties. When energies were presented and revealed en masse like this it complicated matters. The components which went into creating these energies were much more difficult to define. It was almost impossible to single out any specific one. Surrounded by the light and energies of the Goddesses and Celestial Beings, I decided to focus solely on the sacred symbols.

My entire body felt anchored and rooted to the spot. Even supposing I had wanted to, I was incapable of moving so much as a muscle in any direction. I was too enthralled and entranced to be at the very centre of an ever-expanding, spiralling vortex of coloured motion, over which I had absolutely no control. I surrendered myself to the experience.

How long I remained in that particular space and energy is hard to recollect. It might only have been several minutes, but somehow I get a sense of it being longer than that. I do remember quite vividly holding the Staff in my hands and feeling I never wanted to leave this extraordinary place ever again. I wanted to stay there and celebrate being a part of the greater experience. Only later did I realise with any sense of conviction that the entire experience and the outcome had touched some primordial and inherent part of my soul.

Feeling all those energies re-introducing themselves and integrating with my existing energies had a strange effect on me. My mind swelled with liberating sensations and images of rebirth. If anyone had asked a question of me at that exact moment I would have struggled to acknowledge anything and everything about myself. Although cohesive thought had temporarily abandoned me, I knew I had not been abandoned.

With the re-emergence and honouring of ritual and ancient ceremonial came the remembrance. I was reminded and reunited with my past, and given insightful, teasing glimpses of my future. Was I capable of taking and understanding the first step towards that? The answer to that was never in doubt.

part one
the handing over

Just moments before the actual handing over of the Staff, Hathor appeared directly in front of me in all her amazing bovine glory. It was a staggering sight. The sensation of me being diminutive and dwarfed by my surroundings did not lessen in any way. I was aware of the size and dimension of every single thing. In order to accommodate everything that was taking place, the chamber took a deep intake of breath and seemed to expand even further. A disproportionately large temple with solid, carved pillars and a plethora of wide, shallow steps materialised. If belief had not already been suspended, then it certainly was after the emergence of Hathor. It was hard to comprehend that this was actually happening to me. At the same time, I had an unswerving inner conviction'. It definitely was happening. I needed little or no convincing that I should just accept and enjoy this extraordinary experience for what it was. I would be protected. Nothing bad was going to happen, and certainly no harm was going to befall me. I was in a space where only energies of the highest vibrations existed.

If I could have collected my thoughts a little, and secreted a moment of quiet contemplation, I might have reflected upon the significance of Hathor reconnecting with me at that particular moment in time. What had really caught me off guard was the way she appeared before me. Although she and I shared a history spanning many lifetimes, I had never before seen her in her bovine form. She was absolutely resplendent and glorious to look upon.

Her presence in the chamber heralded several immediate changes. Light began to respond by reflecting the energy radiating from her. In an instant, all elements which represented light intensified and magnified a thousand fold. I half expected the light to be blinding, but as it turned out that was not the case. I did not even have to shield my eyes in any way. They adjusted effortlessly to the altering conditions.

Momentum drove events forward. Everything seemed to be on fast forward. All my attention was, not unsurprisingly, focused on Hathor, who stood only a few short feet away from me. My neck arched and my head craned back trying to take in every single facet of her image. Immediately, I reconciled myself to a degree of disappointment. I accepted the futility of capturing and retaining an accurate and definitive image of the bovine majesty before me. If I could slow things down a little then perhaps I might manage to absorb the details more readily. I knew I would not be afforded that particular luxury.

Everything was verging on being too fantastical to fully comprehend. Minute tendrils of uncertainty entered the thought process. For the first time, I began to doubt myself and my own ability to deal with events inside the chamber. Hathor must have caught sense of my inner and physical struggle. Without any effort at all, she lowered her head and brought it in closer to mine. This effectively blocked out every other thing in the chamber. Only she and I existed in that set space. As her eyes drew level with mine I could sense heat emanating from her. That was not all. Some other miraculous thing chose that moment to alert me to its presence. This was something tangible and palpable, and definitely no figment of my imagination. I felt and heard the vibration of a beating heart. I knew it was not my own.

The moment Hathor locked her eyes with mine was utterly compelling and revelatory. It felt as though she had reached right into the very centre of my soul and taken hold. I had never felt more naked in my life. In that split second, she knew everything there was to know about me. She could see me and see my truth. This startling realisation placed me in a state of even further confusion. No one, apart from me, had ever seen my truth. The fact that another could see me with all my faults and foibles was more than a little disconcerting. At some level I did not mind the truth disclosure, but on another level, I knew I probably did. I very quickly accepted that little could be done. All avenues of withdrawal from the hands of another were closed to me. I do not want this to sound like a negative experience. It was not. Even though it was only fleetingly, I felt that any options I might have had had been removed. Hathor's gaze was unflinching, as voluntarily and freely I surrendered my soul into her safe keeping.

I thought my acceptance of that was absolute and unequivocal. What I did not understand was the need to reverse my decision so quickly, and automatically go into self-preservation mode. There was no real reason for me to do that. So much of the essence of me had already been laid bare and revealed to Hathor. Perhaps I just found it difficult to accept that the protective veil, which surrounded all that was me, had finally been removed. It quite literally felt like a ceremonial unveiling. In an afternoon when a new form of reality came knocking I really hoped I could banish the doubts and accept all that was.

I was definitely agitated, yet still alert enough to sense the moment the silent invitation was made. The eye locking had continued. I remember the exact in-breath I was taking when I accepted the much longed for invitation. The compulsion to reach out and touch Hathor's enormous soft toffee-coloured ears became a reality. My hands looked tiny as they sought to stroke the object of so much fascination. Straight away, I could feel how thick and luxurious her coat was, and how bony those ears were just at the point where they met the skull bone. It surprised me a little when I realised something was missing from the image before me. There was no representation of any description depicting the sun disc of Ra. The Goddess's mouth parted and her tongue came out. With the gentlest of touch, she slowly licked my face. Though long and coarsely textured, the sensation from the contact was warm and somehow comforting, and left me feeling nurtured. There was a very real motherly aspect to the contact. Her horns turned out to be smooth and shiny, and looked inordinately heavy. They gave the appearance of stretching out into the stars and infinity beyond. I knew I had to try and reach out and touch them. My hands began gravitating towards them and adapting to the seemingly impossible task. I do not know just how it happened, but somehow I was able to gain some purchase and hold onto Hathor's horns. Though the proportions were completely disproportionate, our faces gently brushed up against one another. This one singular motion triggered something truly astounding.

Our third eyes began to merge. It was a pivotal moment in the entire experience and the one which probably affected me the most. I cannot readily put into words what that felt like. It was extremely complex, yet simplistic at the same time. If I was to try and give a description of the moment then it probably was most like a coming together of all the combined senses and knowledge and knowingness. All the stars in the galaxies reached down and showered me with their brilliance and mystery. Every memory which ever existed opened itself up to me. I was filled with a revival of such compassion and love and understanding of all that WAS and all that IS. It became almost too much for my senses to cope with. I felt consumed and could say no more.

Somewhat incongruously, a flash of a childhood memory chose that moment to step forward. Its absurdity amongst such seriousness broke my concentration, and helped lessen the sense of information and spiritual overload from within. I revisited the joy I knew I had felt when first presented with long, twisting, horn-shaped canes of barley sugar. The child in me had wondered how it was possible to bend and twist sugar until a new elongated shape emerged. In the midst of such a life-changing event, I found myself resurrecting that specific childhood thought.

There was no time at all to ponder my wayward thought. I was about to find out how to do some unusual bending and twisting of my own. With third eyes having merged, Hathor and I rose upwards from the chamber floor, spiralling and twisting, just as the Staff had done only moments before. There was no advanced warning of what would happen next. Without me having to do anything at all, Hathor took control of our energies and our being. I knew the precise moment everything about us seemed to fuse and come together. WE had become ONE.

It may sound naive to say I was astonished by just how heightened my sense of awareness had become, but I really was. For the first time since the sound healing had begun, I was genuinely conscious of the physical and mental. It was an odd sensation. I felt like all my senses had been activated at the same time. Independent of each other, the senses had reached their optimum point. Every fibre and nerve ending in my body was pulsating with the energies of my life force. It was a continuous, free-flowing, almost liquid-like energy. There did not seem to be a beginning or ending to it. A multitude of coloured sparks and electrical impulses shot out from my core. I began to experience having a foothold on the rapid escalator of my life. It felt wonderful.

Up to that point in my journeying, my experience with the great Goddess Hathor had certainly been one of the most profoundly moving spiritual experiences I had ever encountered. It was not over; not just yet, anyway. There was one important thing still to be done. This would be the one thing which would remain with me always and become a major part of me for evermore.

When we ceased moving upwards, from out of nowhere hands appeared and placed the Staff into my hands. It was both a beginning and an ending for me. With a joyful, yet at the same time strangely leaden heart, I faced up to the realisation my experience was drawing to its inevitable close.

part two
after the handing over

My friend and I had shared many spiritual experiences over the years. Neither of us took anything for granted when it came to inviting energies into our own sacred space. We regarded all our encounters and visitations from energies as being something very special indeed. This time around, my friend knew straight away that this experience had been very different for me, and certainly out of the ordinary. She could sense it and see it in my demeanour. Of course, the slightly glazed look on my face was probably the thing which gave it all away.

My friend completed her sound treatment on me. Rather reluctantly, necessity brought me back into my own space. I grounded myself once more and opened my eyes to my earthly reality. The atmosphere in the room was electric and super-charged. I could almost taste it. Still acutely aware of the Staff's energy and vibration, I determined to hold onto those sensations for as long as was humanly possible.

I did not imagine for one minute it would be easy. What I had not bargained on was my inability to grasp any real sense of my own self. There was no recognition at all. A vacuous space where the senses once lived stared back at me. The emotional understandings of only moments ago had retreated. I could not have told you what it was I was feeling, or even how I was feeling. Writing this down makes me realise that that statement is slightly misleading, and not strictly accurate. Some of my senses must have remained, because my mind and body were saturated with feelings and thoughts and sounds. What transpired in those first few moments proved a little disarming and unsettling. I felt incapable of transferring any of those thoughts into intelligible, decipherable language or dialect.

One look at me and any seeing or spiritually aware person would instantly recognise that I had gone through some major event. My friend was smiling at me with that all-knowing look of expectation. 'Well?' she inquired. Was ever one little word drawn out so much, and did it ever have so much meaning?

Time out was needed, and I took it. As always, my friend had great reserves of patience. Slowly, I began the process of trying to put into words my extraordinary experience. My emotions were all over the place. In a physical sense I felt I was still in a state of naked transparency. Whilst I was genuinely excited to be regaling my friend with my astonishing exploits, the transition between other worlds and my perception of my own reality would not make it an easy process. I would need some assistance. Intuitively, I knew I had to call the Staff back to me. I asked my friend to sit down and open herself to connecting with the energies.

The Staff came willingly. My hands were still shaking as I placed the Staff into the outstretched hands of my friend. It was important to me that she should experience the Staff and its astonishing energy first hand. This was too exceptional a gift for me not to share with my closest friend. I could hardly wait to see her reaction to the Staff and its energy.

Initially, the energies in the room seemed to dip a little. They felt weightier and tentative and a little grey. I could feel them all around me, and began to get a real sense of the energies' individual properties. Looking at my friend, I was not so sure she was experiencing the same thing. The energies had yet to reveal themselves to her in the same visual manner of my experience. My friend stated her intentions for the best possible outcome for herself whilst the energies connected with her. I imagined the energies themselves were seeking to determine what those intentions and expectations were. If the Staff presented itself, what did she hope to achieve from her experience with the Staff? Was she happy to open herself up fully to the experience?

You could almost feel the energies and my friend weighing each other up. I can remember thinking at the time how differently the energies were reacting to her. As she began to relax a little and give herself over to the experience, there was a subtle yet definite shift in the way the energy displayed itself. It was a gradual thing. Initially, my friend was bathed in the colours of the Staff's glorious light. Moments later, the energy started to intensify. It began the process of attuning and working directly on her mind. The whole thing lasted about ten or fifteen minutes. She had her own unique experience of the Staff and its energies. Later, she shared her experience with me.

The sensations and experience of the Staff's energies had been powerful. There were no bells and whistles, and bright flashing lights, but something did happen. At some deep, spiritual level my friend got a sense of connection and profound inner peace. We shared something very special that afternoon. Both of us felt incredibly blessed to be a part of something so extraordinary. Though neither of us could possibly have realised it at the time, the Staff would in the years to come play its part in our daily living.

part three
information on the workings of the staff

The experience I have described was not my first experience of that particular chamber, but it was something which changed from being part of visualisations in my head to an event which would become a part of me and my daily workings with the Light. The gift of this Staff brought a strong sense of reconnecting with something both comfortable and familiar. From the very beginning, the message from the Staff was emphatic. It was to be known as the Isis and Hathor Blessing Staff and used solely as an instrument of Blessing. To what degree this differs from (on a personal note I use the coming word so infrequently, but on this occasion so that you can better understand the concept I will use it here) a healing will be down to me to determine in the months and years ahead of me.

Bear with me as I digress momentarily. So as not to confuse you, I should share with you the fact that I had previously been blessed by Spirit with the gift of three other Staffs. Several months separated each gift. Over a period of two to three years the Staffs released (reluctantly at times it has to be said) their properties and powers. It was determined that the first Staff be named the "Oberon Staff "and used for self healing. The second Staff would be known as the "Sirus Staff" and was to be used for Earth healings. The third Staff would be named the "Jupiter Staff "and used for planetary healing.

Because I had had the Blessing Staff in my possession for the shortest period of time, it was obviously the one I knew least well, and therefore the one that had still to reveal its capabilities and potential to the same degree as the others. From the outset, I knew it was going to take a lot of time and energy to try and unravel its mysteries and better understand its workings. Where to start? What to ask? Recurring questions that initially existed were: What or who were the recipients of the Blessing to be? What purpose would the Blessing serve? How did the Staff and its givers/creators intend for me to carry out their intentions? What was the Blessing and would I recognise it when I saw and heard it? As with the previous Staffs, the answers to these, or indeed any of my questions, were not easily accessed. There were no clues or guidelines as to just how to proceed. I was left to wrestle with my thoughts for a long time.

As there was no real direction as to how to put the Staff to use, I started off proceedings by opting to give myself a Blessing from the Staff. Consciously focusing on slowing down my breathing and stilling my wandering thoughts, I called the Staff to me. With both hands, I reached out and attempted to hold the Staff aloft over my reclining body. My initial close-up observations were ... the Staff was broad and flat and several inches thick. I was struck immediately by its enormous weight, and by the constant flow of energy spiralling and twisting its way up the long central column of the Staff. A large percentage of the Staff was taken up with six solid heart shapes which covered it. Only the lower section of the column was left exposed. This allowed the energy to be shown in effortless, free-flowing motion. It was a truly magnificent sight, and instantly had me spellbound. One other component contributed to the Staff and made it whole. At the very top of the column, directly above the six original hearts already mentioned, another solid individual heart rested upon two upturned cobras' heads. As my hands sought to secure tenure of the Staff, this marginally larger heart seemed to me to be the easiest way of actually holding onto an item of such awkward dimensions and design. It felt strange at first, but as I gazed at the object in my hands that quickly passed. The wood the Staff was made of was beautiful and smooth to touch. Made entirely of burnished glistening ebony, this Staff was definitely the heaviest of all the Staffs I had been gifted. Perhaps it contained more content and therefore more complexities? At that point, I just did not know. What I could tell and see with my own eyes was that this newly acquired gift pulsated and vibrated with Energy, Light, and Life.

No words were spoken in blessing, but the energy and sensations pouring into and around my body spoke volumes. As I held the Staff between my hands, immediately I got the sense of being back in that incredible vortex of symbols. It probably took a little longer than it should have. The moment of discovering the real identity of the symbols finally dawned. THEY were the Blessing.

Colours came and went. I became conscious of the physical. The Staff became heavier and heavier, and the strain on my arms increased. This struck me as decidedly odd. No previous form of energy work had had that effect on me or my body. Using intention as a means of directing energy was normally effortless. It was a tried and tested way of working with energies. However, it was of no assistance at all in this particular set of circumstances. It soon became apparent that this was going to require a physical contribution from me just to hold onto the Staff and use it. I was not at all sure how to sustain the exacting usage of the Staff if I was in a weakened physical state. I need not have worried. The Staff looked after me. There came a point when I knew I could no longer hold onto the Staff or its energies. I took that as a sign that the Blessing was complete.

Since that date I have used the Blessing a couple of times in conjunction with the Jupiter Staff (see drawing opposite). Whilst the Staff gave its Blessing freely about dual usage, it is not what it is intended for. I have recently been given information about the six heart shapes that form the greater part of the Staff. They represent the continents. When the Staff is in use, each heart shape projects a colour which can and will change, depending on specific needs or circumstances. At present, the colours are fourth dimensional, but can change in an instant to fifth dimensional. I mention this aspect of the Staff purely because of my experiences and its relevancy to me and my usage of the Staff. It may well be entirely different for another person using the Staff. Colours might play a more or less significant role when the Blessing is in use. I don't honestly know. At this point, I am still trying to find my way.

Isis & Hathor offer me assistance and guidance when I seek it. These two extraordinary powers were responsible for creating the Blessing within this precious Staff. It is up to each recipient of the Staff and its Blessing to decipher and understand its true meaning in relation to them. By creating and delivering such a Blessing into the safe keeping of others, Isis and Hathor are bestowing something entirely unique and restorative to this universe of ours. Whichever way you choose to look at this, that is something huge. At least it is in my eyes, anyway.

Being given the unique opportunity to learn and work with a phenomenal energy is exceptional. By entrusting us with this gift, the energies are effectively declaring that we are the ones who will bring necessary changes to the world. The energies must have a tremendous amount of faith in our abilities to carry out their wishes.

I can tell you from experience, carrying out this work will test you on many levels. Whoever gives the Blessing will need to be focused and patient. A certain degree of courage and self-belief will be required. You will be tested and challenged along the way. If you allow yourself to be guided by the Staff, those challenges should not prove insurmountable.

One of the first things to be aware and clear about is just exactly what will be expected when the Staff and the Blessing are in use. It would be very easy to let our own expectations of the Staff enter the

Recent Short Self Healing
from Blessing Staff

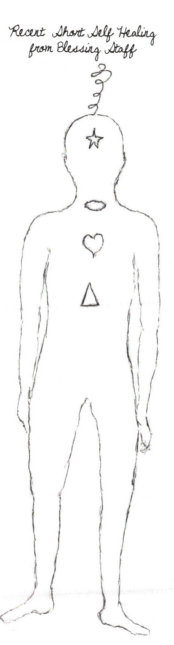

The crown

Large spiraling
rainbow crystal
connects the energy
and consciousness of
self to the Higher
Dimensions.

Throat

An oval pale aqua
crystal reminds me
of the strength of
dolphin energy and its
connection to Atlantis.

Solar Plexus

This Pyramid of
energy is a deep sea
green colour. It sits at
the centre of all that
is me and drives me
to accept and convey all
that is good.

Third eye

Indigo / Midnight Blue
covered with smattering
of brilliant stars.
Reactivates strong
connection with my
'Star' ancestors and
gives me the strength
to continue to work
amongst them.

Heart

This feels solid to the
touch. It is magenta in
colour reminding me of
the energy of Mary.
Everytime I see this
colour I am comforted.
The odd thing about
this particular heart is
the curled fossilised
invertebrate at its
centre. This heart
is about remembering
Ancient deeds and
knowledge.

This intense Blessing /
healing affected only five
chakra points. Each point had
a specific symbol + colour.

83

equation and muddy the waters, so make a conscious effort not to allow this to happen. Time is an essential component for a successful outcome, so again make sure you take time. Whatever you do, don't feel compelled to rush things, and don't be afraid to ask for guidance from Source. Remind yourself frequently to recognise the complexity of the energy. Learn to accept that the Staff dictates the outcome of a successful Blessing. It will guide you to the exact location where the Blessing is most needed on the day. There may be times when the energy might demonstrate a reluctance to reveal itself. When that happens, never try to force the issue or see it as anything negative. If the Blessing is not appropriate on that day, then there will always be other opportunities.

the individual hearts + their meaning

So far, what I have discovered about this energy is this; each heart/ continent has to deal with matters relating specifically to that continent. In order that no confusion attaches itself to this: I am not talking about what some might regard as conventional healing, for example physical, distance, Earth, planetary and so on (though at a later date these might play their part). The Blessing Staff deals with the emotions and living attitudes of a continent. It deals with man's greed, hunger for power, prejudices, influence, affluence, poverty, bigotry, racism, ostracism, corruption, collusion, hatred; the list is endless. It is not a question of holding the Staff aloft and suddenly all of Africa or Asia is cured of all negative aspects attributed to that particular continent. Nor should it be expected that one sweep of the Blessing to the numerous countries involved in drug or people trafficking will resolve those utterly insidious issues overnight. It quite simply doesn't work like that.

If you are anything like me I am sure you will be asking yourself 'How on Earth do I make a start on something like that?' Because the scale of the task is so colossal, how is it possible to establish who, what or which has the greatest need and urgency? How can I even think of tackling something which is so difficult to actually define? Do I start at the top of what I perceive to be openly corrupt governments and their officials, or do I make a start in the back streets where another type of corruption and collusion is taking place? Should I single out the sick, the needy or the homeless? Would it be better if I focused my energies and concentrated on the millions of displaced persons who live in squalor and are deprived of even their most basic human rights? Will there ever be the remotest chance of starvation being eradicated? Can any real inroads be made into religious intolerance? Would people really care anyway if I took that particular stance?

When I took my first tentative steps into how I could best use the Blessing, I very soon realised that the task ahead was gigantic, and that sooner rather than later, I was going to need some help. There were times when using the Staff I felt as though I was drowning in a quagmire of darkness and liquid slime. I had to rise swiftly to the surface in order to breathe in the fresh air of survival. The one thought which did sustain me, and kept me from going under and failing the task ahead of me, was the challenge of making a real difference even if it was one tiny step at a time.

The message from the Blessing states that the time is ripe NOW for reuniting the continents. They have to learn before it is too late to heal and come together again through love. Each heart/continent has a beat. The large independent heart at the top of the Staff is the Master Heart and represents love around the world. It will reunite all with its power and Blessings (combined with the Blessings of the individual continents). Together, we can help facilitate that and bring it into being NOW.

I have worked with the Staff for a considerable time now, and I never cease to be amazed by the beauty, the power and the sheer glory of the energy contained within the Staff's Blessing. Without going completely over the top about the Staff, I do feel incredibly privileged to have been chosen as a guardian of The Isis and Hathor Blessing Staff. To be the first recipient of an energy which will help restore balance, unity and love to humanity as a whole is a very special gift. I will certainly do my best to pass my knowledge on the workings of the Staff to other recipients, in the knowledge that, as one, we will make that final and lasting difference.

Extract no. 5:
Past life experiences

Most of us spend at least a quarter, if not a third, of each day sleeping. If you add all those hours up in human years, no matter which way you look at it, that is a scary amount of 'living' time spent in a state of slumber. I am a great advocate for sleep. I love the sensation of slipping gently from the reality of the day into the dream state of the invitational night. My dreams tend to be remarkably ordinary extensions of everyday life experiences or occasional fantastical forays into the subconscious mind.

As I set out on my spiritual path I continue to dream away the night hours. The only difference is my interpretation of my dreams becomes more insightful. During the early stages of my journey I sense a real fundamental shift in consciousness taking place. As strange and as dramatic as this sounds it has the affect of appearing to alter aspects of my thought process and redefine elements of my brain patterning. To me, this is never more evident than in moments when both the body and the mind become still and settle into a state of deep spiritual meditation. There is an innate awareness and knowing of something at the very core of my existence being reactivated and set in motion.

I learn to really listen to the resurgence of my intuitive senses. Paying close attention enables me to make sure I hear what my intuition is telling me. I accept this deepened and heightened meditative state is no dream state. In so many cases it triggers the start of ancient memory and past lives being reawakened and brought back into the present. I welcome those parts of me and embrace them for what they are.

Below are several, though by no means all, of those past lives.

the bonds of slavery

The last words to pass my lips every night have a certain predictability and resonance to them. Their content and tone seldom, if ever, varies. On my knees in front of God I pray that history will not repeat itself and I will not have to endure such deprivation and hardship ever again. I bargain and promise my God so much in return, but he does not hear my voice or my words. It is wrong of me to suppose I can place all my faith and dreams of freedom into his hands.

Once again, my body struggles to adapt to the solid inflexible structure and weight of the iron chains scraping against my ankles. There is little I can do to protect myself from the incessant chaffing of already bloodied skin. How many bodies have been weighed down by the exact same chains now enslaving me? I wonder. As soon as my mind goes there I stop it in its tracks. It will not do me any good or serve any purpose to continue along those lines. I must not allow myself to think of such things. Instead of ruminating over the destinies of others, I must concentrate on myself and my own survival. In a way, I am luckier than many of the other slaves. Worn down by the ravages of lengthy enslavement, many have simply lost the will to live and as a result have handed their souls over to their maker. Although I have been treated harshly, I still have youth and health on my side. Surely that will stand me in some stead?

What little energy I have is used in trying to remain standing upright as gravity drags my body downwards. It is not easy being shackled and in chains. I chastise myself for visiting my own misery. Why should it matter if it is easy or not? I am an indentured slave with no entitlements of any description. Being a slave about to be shipped off to my new owner I have a monetary value. In the eyes of those who have enslaved me that is what defines me as a person. As a human being bound by the chains of servitude, I am of no value at all.

Natural light is in short supply and the ventilation is poor. The stench of bodies pervades everything. There is no getting away from it. So much flesh, sweating and sweltering in crammed conditions, threatens at times to become almost too much to bear. In some extreme cases it is too much to bear. Two of the slaves have died already from heat exhaustion and dehydration. The slave master is not happy seeing his profits slip through his fingers like that. Those days turn out to be really bad for those who have survived. Many feel guilt at having survived, whilst just as many again feel cheated not to be chosen to escape the purgatory of a life without freedom.

Even in death, the recently departed are paid little or no regard. Their lifeless forms lay on the spot where they expire. Those poor, unfortunate souls are left for hours chained to the person next to them until such time as the bodies can be dragged out and thrown overboard. No words or ceremony are conducted in recognition of a life lived. Whenever I think of those so recklessly tossed aside I determine that will not be the way I end up. Those are the nights I pray a little longer and speak a little louder to God.

The voyage seems to go on forever, with one day blurring and merging into the next. Many of the slaves have endured lengthy periods of sea sickness. Their brows are weighted and furrowed with sweat, and their eyes plead for someone somewhere to help them. On top of everything else, they have to cope with the remorseless bouts of incessant nausea, which leave them in an extremely weakened state. I lose track of the number of times I begin to wonder if any of us will ever set foot on land again. The conditions below deck continue to be insufferable. We all know that is the way it is and we learn to suffer in silence. Those who cannot, or do not, adhere to the code of silence are singled out as troublemakers. Depending on the mood of the slave master on the day, sometimes a heavy duty collar is placed around the necks of those vociferous souls before they are beaten down into total submission.

After several weeks sailing the high seas, the slave master makes the decision to remove the chains from a group of slaves. I am at a loss to understand why I am one of the slaves chosen. Again, I remind myself that in the reality which is my life at this time I do not have to understand it. I know I probably should feel guilty for being chosen, but I do not. Inside my heart is dancing and rejoicing. I am thankful to be free from the chains of slavery, no matter how short a time it might turn out to be.

Ludicrous as it may seem, I always feel I have one advantage over my enslavers. Something which always remains elusive to my captors and exclusive to me are the thoughts I have. No chains enslave them, and more importantly, no one apart from me has access into or control over them. It almost feels like a victory of sorts to be holding onto something of my own.

The slave master is only feet away. In his hand he holds a weighty set of keys. He approaches and, reaching down, grabs hold of my chains. How I long to take hold of those chains and strangle him, but of course I cannot and I do not. I stare at his glistening, bald head instead. Beads of sweat form and begin a steady trickle. The slave master is overweight and out of condition, and it shows. Even the small task of bending is an effort. Leaning over me, I can see the muscles at the back of his neck begin to crease and bulge. The excess flesh has no place to go. It is grotesque watching flesh folding in upon flesh. Even as I turn my head away, there is no way to avoid the strong, stale odour of his body. I keep expecting him to change his mind, but he does not. He turns the key and yanks at my ankle chains before moving off towards another fortunate.

Releasing my chains triggers a host of emotions. I cannot stop my thoughts from returning to the day of the slave market. I have just been sold on to a new master. Hundreds of slaves from all four corners of the world are auctioned off that day. We are an odd assortment of human flesh. Not all have dark skin and hair like me. Some are small and pale skinned. Others are olive skinned and have strange markings and colourings on their bodies. There is even an albino amongst us. He attracts a great deal of attention and fetches a good price. Once the auction is concluded, it does not take long to round up this seething mass of humanity. We are herded like cattle from the abattoirs onto a huge ship before quickly being taken below deck and manacled and chained to each other.

That is the last ray of sun any of us see for a long time. None of us know where we are going, but some of us have an understanding of what lies ahead. I have been sold before and I know my life will continue in a downward spiral. I have no control at all of what is happening to me, and what is likely to happen to me in the future. Memory rears its head and reminds me it is unlikely to be a good or positive experience. Somewhere deep within, however, rests a defiant spirit. A little voice keeps telling me that I must hold onto life, no matter how horrendous it turns out to be. I determine that I can and will survive everything that is thrown at me. Those are the words and thoughts that keep me moving forward with the wretchedness of my life.

Whatever the reasons, I am free of the chains. It feels strange taking a step without the expected dragging or friction. Only a dozen or so slaves have been chosen. There is no time to even think about why I am one of the selected few. Along with the others, I am pushed and prodded towards the steps leading to the deck above. The hatch directly overhead is released from the rusted bolts and chains that hold it in place. Suddenly, light comes flooding in. Those still anchored and bound by chains turn their heads towards the light now streaming down upon them. It must be absolute torture to be teased by the light, only to have it blocked out again moments later when the hatch is secured once more.

I attempt to follow the man in front of me, but his height and size are more of a hindrance than an asset. He is huge in stature and girth. I cannot remember ever seeing anyone as tall as him. His thighs are muscled and defined. Former lashings have left their trademark scarring across his back and his shoulders. His spine is ramrod straight and he is as broad as an ox. Because space is so restricted he has real difficulty keeping his balance. Every time he takes a step his feet keep slipping off the worn down treads. So it is I find myself stumbling, rather than climbing, my way up the narrow wooden treads in the footsteps of former slaves. I have to shield my eyes as I catch my first sighting of sunlight in over a month. Finally, I reach the last wooden tread separating below deck from above deck. My bare feet secure their first free grip on the surface of the coarse planked decking. What a feeling it is.

I stand to one side with a couple of other slaves. We watch as at least a dozen more faces emerge from the hell hole below. For some reason unknown to me at the time, I make the conscious decision to stay still slightly apart from the man I followed up the stairs. Because he is a bit of a rarity amongst the slaves everyone notices him. My natural instinct is to try and make myself look as inconspicuous as possible. It will not do to stand out in any way.

The deck is gigantic and a hive of disciplined industry. There is so much to see and take in. I have no idea how many deckhands the ship has, but from those I can initially see, they number several dozen. The noise on deck surprises me. When the wind catches the vast canvas sails the sound overrides everything else. Work for the deckhands looks hard and dangerous, yet they take it all in their stride. They are continually harangued. Constant attention is paid to the barrage of voices barking out a steady stream of orders. For a time, deckhands stop what they are doing in order to stare. We are well used to people reacting in this way. The expression on the faces of the deckhands speaks volumes. Some find it hard to conceal the disgust they feel towards the enslavers whilst others' indifference towards our plight is apparent. Many find it impossible to hold eye contact with us and have to look away. No words of abuse or condemnation pass their lips. In their heart of hearts, every one of them recognises the humiliation and degradation all the slaves are forced to endure. It would be hard not to. Silence falls over everything. Only the sound of the ship cutting a passage through the waves can be heard. That state of affairs does not last for long. Whoever is in charge soon gets the deckhands back to work again.

Each of us is given a measure of water from a container which looks a little like an upside down turtle shell. Though the measure is frugal, we drink thirstily. None of us have any idea what will happen next. We are moved to the stern and told to stand and wait. There is no hardship in this. It gives all of us time to take in our surroundings and breathe in the fresh, tropical air. The wind against our face is steady and brings some relief from the ferocious sun. Particles of sea spray carried on the wind reach out and land on my feet.

I do not know what the other slaves are thinking, but I am frightened of being on this ship in this ocean. It is so vast and does not appear to have either a beginning or an ending. Even the sky seems to lose itself in the never-ending expanse of tidal motion. I keep looking out for signs of land, but cannot catch glimpse of anything. Occasionally, tiny specks might appear to break the distant horizon, but those speculative sightings rarely amount to anything.

We are still standing on deck a couple of hours later. As soon as I see the slave master and a group of young officers involved in a heated argument I know something is wrong. Somewhere, a link in the chain of command has broken down. There is a great deal of shouting and pointing in our general direction. The louder the officers shout, the more inflexible and intractable the slave master becomes. Without warning, the argument escalates. In a matter of seconds the verbal altercation turns physical. Although the slave master is outnumbered, he stands his ground and refuses to yield to anyone. Seeing an opportunity for dissent, several of the deckhands decide to switch allegiance and join in. It only takes that one spark of indiscipline to ignite further fighting. Rank is disregarded and control of the ship begins to slide. I do not quite believe what I am seeing. How will this all end? I ask myself. My mind goes into overdrive and takes off in all directions. The fighting is in full swing. Surely it is only a question of time before arms are released from the armoury. Can I somehow use this distraction to my advantage? What, if anything, can I gain from the situation?

Just before the ruckus on deck started I noticed a minuscule spit of land. Though it is a couple of miles or so away, it catches my attention. Thoughts that should remain dormant begin to take shape in my mind. It takes only seconds for visions of escape to infiltrate my brain. I know it is madness to be encouraging such ridiculous imaginings, but I do not seem able to help myself. The wheels of thinking the impossible are suddenly set in motion. Within the confines of my mind this is as dangerous a game as I will ever play in my entire life. Wanting something badly enough often transcends improbability and human logic. Justifying the impossible therefore comes easily. There is no escaping the alarm bells going off in my head, yet I still continue to give free rein and power to thoughts of escape. Although the spit is no more than a dot in the distance, it is definitely sending out signals that invite further investment of time and thought. I can feel the energy of the spit reach out and pull me straight towards it.

The biggest question of my life stares me in the face. It shows no signs of retreating or going away and needs an answer. Should I listen to my heart, which is screaming out one thing, or should I listen to my head, which is yelling something else? I am so confused, I do not know what to do.

Conscious not to draw attention to that confusion, I swiftly avert my eyes and try projecting an air of casual indifference. I am foolish to believe no one will notice my deception. Someone on deck has and he is letting me know. The slave stares at me with complete incredulity and disbelief. Without uttering one single syllable, his eyes convey every single thing he is thinking. Inside, I feel panic rise and lodge in my throat. I am sure the slave can sense that panic. Our gazes lock, with neither of us prepared to give way. At this moment, I feel as if we are the only two people in the entire universe. In the end, it is me who breaks the connection.

I still do not really believe I am actually giving credence to the thoughts currently thrusting and parrying inside my head. Don't I know I can be flogged for trying to escape? People have been put to death for less. Have I learnt nothing about the lives of slaves over the years?

The pull towards the spit of land is strong. I feel it cast its net wide and wrap itself around me. Trying to call a halt to scenes being enacted in my head becomes nigh on impossible. Visions of my imminent escape from the drudgery of slavery just keep on coming and forcing their way through. I try to rationalise the demons in my head. In the end I give up trying. I have to accept that this might be the only chance I might ever have of escaping.

When the fights on board start some deeply suppressed emotion inside me rushes forward demanding to be recognised. I give it the recognition it demands. To me, it feels in some strange way as if destiny is stepping in to offer a helping hand. The plan, such as it is, does not take long to lay down its roots. Knowing the risks involved still is not enough of a deterrent to stop me from exploring the possibilities of my hastily evolved plan. Several times, I question my sanity. Is there a realistic probability of escaping? Surely I am not really thinking I can just slip silently over the side of the ship and into the water and swim away to the spit of land without being noticed? It will be incredibly dangerous attempting such a thing. I can end up having my body smashed against the side of the ship. If that does not kill me then the power of the waves lifting me up and tossing me around surely will. The more I think about it, the more desperate and panicked I become. In the end, I convince myself that everything will miraculously turn out in my favour.

One thing is holding me back from a full-blown commitment. No matter how badly I might wish otherwise, this is not something I can ignore or imagine disappearing into thin air. I do not know whether it is fate or chance which drew my eyes towards the dark outline of something just beneath the surface of the waves. Although it is a short distance away from the ship, I intuitively know the shape is a large shark. My thoughts return to my childhood. I can remember how I longed to set out with the men of my village to track sharks which swam into the shallower birthing waters. Before I reached maturity and could share in that experience, the slavers came and took me away. Many know the saying "once seen, never forgotten". The same is true for me. I can still recognise the shape of a shark anywhere.

The sighting is brief, but I cannot remove the image of it from my brain. I know what my eyes have seen. If I need further confirmation of the fact then the fin slicing effortlessly through the water before rising above the surface of a wave proves my point exactly. Panic really does then take hold. It rages quite uncontrollably through my body. What can I do? I have to forcibly prise the question out of myself. Is this a lone shark or are others lying in wait? Shall I make my bid for freedom knowing a shark patrols the waters between me and the distant spit? I know I am a strong swimmer, but can I survive a swim of that length and that danger? So many questions remain unresolved, but I do not have the luxury of time on my side to resolve them. The time is now. Am I ready to commit to escape or not?

I know I only have a short window of opportunity to carry out my plan. If my plan fails and I am caught, little mercy will be shown. The punishment meted out will be swift. As soon as I say this to myself I realise for about the thousandth time in my life the absurdity of my thoughts. My life as a free man IS effectively over. What else is there for me to lose? Propping myself up with brave words of fighting a good fight, and staying alive at all costs, are meaningless and have a hollow ring to them. If I cannot be free of my life of enslavement, what exactly am I staying alive for? I was taken from my homeland and torn from whatever family I knew. Anyone who ever mattered to me has probably imagined I am already dead. Until I am free of everything which binds me to my present life I will never taste freedom again. I do not need any further convincing. It is time to try to free my life for myself.

If I stand any chance at all of escaping, I know I am going to have to be bold and take hold of my own destiny. I cannot allow myself to think what will happen if things go wrong.

With so much fighting and distraction on board it is easier than I imagine. Crouching down and concealing myself under the small cannons of the ship has gone without a hitch. I cannot believe I have not been noticed. Moving my head gives me my first close up view of the sea below. I feel physically sick looking down. My conservative guess of the drop is at least fifty or sixty feet. The waves are enormous and much more menacing and life threatening than I imagine. Thoughts of sharks are nothing as compared to this. Should I or shouldn't I?

There is never really any doubt in my mind what I do next. Regardless of who might see, I position myself to squeeze through the cannon opening and into the ocean below. At this point fate lends another helping hand. The slave who has a knowing of what I am about to do is much steadier on his feet now. He comes and stands with his back towards me. No one really notices when his enormous frame blocks out the sight of my crouching form. It is up to me now to make my escape.

I hit the water with such tremendous force I think my escape is over before it has begun. Will I be able to survive the initial dive into the ocean? The waves are so powerful and my body so momentarily shocked I have to fight to keep my head above the waves. As the waves rise and fall, they keep sucking me under, threatening to fill my lungs in the process. Survival mode kicks in and my arms and legs automatically begin to move in a forward motion. I start to propel my body away from the swell of the ship's wake and towards the tiny pinprick of land and what I hope will be freedom. The expectation of gunshot and voices raised in alarm remain a constant and almost overriding fear, but none ever come. Keeping my strokes to a steady rhythm, I swim and swim. At one point I see shark fins some distance away. They terrify me.

I am sure I have been in the water for hours, yet the spit of land does not seem to be getting any closer. The fight and determination I showed earlier is beginning to ebb. I am conscious of the salt water in my nostrils and mouth as I struggle to stay afloat. My eyes are taking a relentless pounding as I continue my battle against the seething cauldron of foam and spray. Several times, I almost succumb and go under. The battle for final ownership of my life begins. I rally and rage at life itself. How much more am I expected to endure? Thoughts of giving up and handing my body over to the lair of Neptune on the ocean's floor are always present. Something always stops me from doing that. I only have to think of the eyes of the slave who has helped me. So long as I have breath in my lungs I will not surrender my life to the ocean.

My body is depleted in every way and unable to absorb the oxygen it needs to sustain it. On the cusp of complete physical and mental exhaustion, I lose my sense of focus and direction. I may even begin to hallucinate a little. One of the last things I remember seeing before I drift into a semi comatose state is the outline of elongated fins closing in and beginning to circle me. Perhaps my ending will come by way of the ocean after all? I almost defy the world to make it so. The very last thing I remember is shouting out for God to hear my words and help me.

I know I am alive because I can hear and feel my heart beating softly and steadily against the sand beneath me. Water is lapping around my ankles moving in and out between my toes. I try to raise myself up on one elbow but fail miserably and my head falls forward and lands on my bloodied forearm. Just before my eyes close again, I see the curve of the long beach stretching away from me.

The sun is lower in the sky when I next wake up. My body remonstrates against the battering it has endured. This time, when I try to move further up the beach, I am successful. This time, I am able to take in everything around me. I cannot stop staring at the miracle of my life. I have survived and made it to the spit of land! At first, I do not believe it. I am safe on the shifting sands of terra firma once more! Reality rapidly infuses my senses, filling me and my heart with peace and unrestrained elation. God has heard me calling out to him after all. Only HE in his grace could have picked my exhausted body up out of the ocean and carried it to a place of safety. I look up to the heavens and give thanks to God for my life. That is when I breathe out and allow the first tears of my long awaited freedom to flow.

at the court of louis xiv

All the excavations and recent extensions to the gardens have been well worth the wait. In an era where opulence and extravagance reign, I still cannot recall seeing anything so breathtaking or so flamboyant in style. The army of gardeners who carried out this magnificent architectural vision had excelled themselves. Everywhere the eyes come to rest, flowers of every description stand in regimented glory, dazzling with their kaleidoscopic colours. Every time I breathe in I am caressed by a heady profusion of the floral notes filling the air. The gardens more than do justice to the palace they deem to represent. Soon, the whole world will hear about the famous Gardens of Versailles.

It has not always been so, but today I find myself smiling at the sheer frivolity and jollity of life at the court of King Louis XIV of France. Being of noble birth myself, I am accustomed to feeling at home in such surroundings. Although my connection to the King is distant it is nonetheless recognised as being of some import. From an early age, my position amongst the social elite is never in doubt.

An air of expectancy hangs over everything as hundreds of people stroll in the afternoon sunlight, awaiting the arrival of their Sun King. It seems to me as though every nobleman in Paris has travelled to Versailles, complete with personal entourages, for the grand occasion. Considering their often precocious and fickle natures, few, if any, can fail to be impressed by the lavishness of their surroundings. All the upheaval of the King moving his entire court to Versailles has won the day and quelled his doubters.

As with so many things involving the courtiers to the King, a definite sense of intrigue and high drama attaches itself to the occasion. People quite literally jockey for position, seeking to gain maximum vantage in such illustrious circles. There is a definite social hierarchy. Once the seal of acceptance is granted, select personages come together in intimate groups in order to gossip and contrive. People are always conscious not to be overheard. If the courtiers were not so blatantly obvious about who to include or exclude, their actions might even be considered amusing. Many at court find the whispering and conversations cut short as they approach distasteful and ill mannered. There is a great deal of political and courtly posturing going on. Much as I hate myself for doing so, I find the intrigue hard to ignore.

The afternoon is filled with chattering voices and a great deal of polite laughter. Everyone is in good spirits. Gentlemen in wigs pose and feign apparent indifference, as pampered ladies parade leisurely in all their finery, each trying to outdo the other. Some succeed. People marvel at the costumes and carnival atmosphere. Performers are everywhere. Entertainers walk precariously on wooden stilts, whilst clowns try to amuse their jaded audiences. Musicians enthral with their instruments. Exotic animals, never intended to inhabit the slightly cooler climes of France, pull at the chains that bind them as circus children walk on rigid aerial wires directly above them. There is so much to see and hear. The atmosphere is joyful and infectious.

All the ladies have planned their wardrobe well in advance of the grand opening of the gardens. Their seamstresses and dressmakers have been working feverishly on the fashionable gowns for months. Many seek silent acclaim and recognition of how well they are dressed. Others hope their latest creation will set them apart from the beauties of the day. One of the greatest accolades will, of course, be if the King singles any of them out for attention. I find it all immensely amusing. It isn't just the ladies seeking approval. The gentlemen are equally vain.

I have chosen to wear a gown of my finest silk, mirroring the colour of the sky above me. The gown is stunning and incredibly delicate, and draws attention to my slender waist. It fits me to absolute perfection. The bodice of the dress has been embroidered with golden threads from the Orient and encrusted with hundreds of beautiful little seed pearls, each one individually sewn on by hand. It is a truly exquisite gown, and much admired.

The day is going well. For no reason at all, the joyful feeling I experienced earlier begins to dissipate. Alarm bells, so quiet of late, suddenly go off in my head. I can feel the joy rapidly slipping away from me. Before I can even attempt to reach out and catch hold of that feeling again, the stranglehold on my senses and emotions becomes my new reality. Its grip is so tight and suffocating I find myself barely able to catch my breath. Because I have similar experiences to this in the past, I know what to expect. It is never a good experience and does not bode well for a serene and calm ending to this special day. I ask myself why here of all places, and why now in front of so many people? If I allow events to escalate any further, and do not manage to wrestle back control of the situation, there is the very real likelihood of this being my final attendance at court. Whilst that aspect of social exclusion does not worry me to any real degree, I still do not wish to draw attention to myself and have it happen like this.

There is no time left to try and do anything about it. The mortification and panic I am enduring immediately manifests itself in cheeks which feel as though they are on fire. I sense everyone has noticed and pray this is not so. Raising my fan helps to hide a little of my physical discomfort.

Ignoring my predicament in the unfolding drama is never an option. The reality of my situation begins sinking in. What makes it even worse is the realisation that this is not just about me and what is happening to me. There is a great deal more at stake than social embarrassment. Etiquette demands I will have to get through this somehow, without causing offence and embarrassment to the King. Trying to regain some semblance of control over my emotional collapse is a humiliating and daunting prospect. If only the ground could hear my pleas and open up beneath me.

I know I am falling back into that gaping black hole of despair once more. How can this be happening again, after years fighting so incredibly hard to escape it? There is not one solitary thing I can call upon to halt the torturous and relentless pace of my advance into that dark space. I cannot believe God is so cruel as to force me to face it all over again.

Memories of three separate childbirths crash mercilessly towards me, saturating my mind with images guaranteed to inflict the greatest pain. I close my eyes, trying to shield myself from the agony of it all. The passage of time has failed me yet again. Nothing can lessen my grief. It never really ever goes away. The images are raw and cling to me, threatening to consume me with their intensity. All three of the deliveries ended in still births. Every single death led to the absolute desolation and destruction of my soul. Whilst I knew I could possibly recover from the physical memories, the emotional and mental memories all but destroyed me. Only the love of my husband helped me through those dark, troubled times. Together, we struggled to cope with the void of desolation left by the deaths of our newborns. Sharing our grief did not always work. If my beautiful husband had not been so loving and sensitive and understanding I doubt very much if I would have survived at all.

My husband is dead now, taken by the very heart which had given so selflessly. When he needed it the most, his heart failed to recover from experiencing too much pain. Since that final crushing blow, it has taken years for me to try and move forward with my life again. Although the grief I feel at the death of my husband is incalculable, somehow I manage to continue to move forward with living my life.

The pain where my heart lays is back with a fury which almost defies description. It is so intense and gripping now, I fear I will pass out from the force and magnitude of it. I long to move away, but find I am unable to do so. My feet are leaden and deeply rooted to the soil beneath my jewelled slippers. The tentacles of loss reach out and extinguish any thought of recovery. I can feel the utter panic rise up inside me and nausea sweep through every particle of my being. I know I have to get away from here before my legs buckle beneath me. "Dear God in heaven" I scream in my head." Will someone please help me?"

My eyes fall upon the figure of a man standing some distance from me. I have no recollection of having noticed him before. He is taller than most men and projects a certain air of silent serenity. In the sunlight his hair looks burnished and golden. He is a strikingly handsome man. Dressed in the palest blue silk just like me, it is impossible not to notice this man. A thought flashes briefly through my mind. I sense we are almost dressed to complement each other somehow. What an odd thought it is. There is something about the man that is even more disconcerting. He is looking directly at me.

I do not know if my imagination is playing tricks on me or not. Apart from his physical attributes, something else about this man makes him stand out from those around him. He has a presence which is difficult to define. I cannot take my eyes off him. Who is he and how long has he been watching me? I wonder. It is impossible to break the eye contact. Even if I could, I do not really want to. Although I do not fully understand it, I intuitively know this man is important to me. He is here to help me.

The pain in my heart and my head has never been as excruciating as it is right at this moment. If I could rip the pain out of me I would. I have reached the end of the road and know I cannot carry this burden any further. Living another moment with this torment is more than I can endure. It is cutting off the very breath of my being. My heart is wracked and stretched with so much undiluted pain, it is now on the point of disintegrating.

My eyes are still locked with the eyes of the man. Mine plead and beg him to understand the battle of hopelessness and abandonment raging within me. I need so much from this man. Is he capable of giving me that? Right at this moment, it is important for me to know whether he will be there to catch me if I fall through the gaps in my reality. I want him to be able to see and understand the emptiness in my heart. Just as soon as I think that thought, something strange begins to happen. The only way I can describe it is by saying that everything going on around me takes on a dream, almost trance-like, state. Sound melts away entirely and stillness wraps itself around every living thing. The beautiful gardens and the fashionable people inhabiting that space slowly fade away into the background. Only two people are left standing.

A soft reflective cloud of luminous light separates us. I know it will not be for long. Never once does the man allow his gaze to falter. He walks towards me covering the distance in seconds. Now he is standing in front of me, I can sense his extraordinary sensitivity and power. The intensity and depth of colour of his eyes is hypnotic. They draw me in so deeply I can feel myself begin to merge with his energy. That is when I know I can trust this man absolutely and hand all of myself over to his care.

Slowly, and with the gentlest touch, my would be saviour reaches out and draws my hands into his. No words are spoken, but the communication which takes place has profound meaning for me. Instantly, my thoughts calm along with my anxiety. The sensations his touch invokes make me want to cry. He holds me tenderly as the floodgates open and tears begin to flow. Memories of a soul lost to grief slowly release their hold and begin to wash away. I think my body will break as I cry as I have never cried before. We stand there for the longest time. Slowly my tears halt and I begin to feel I am coming alive again. Light is filtering into my soul.

When it is over, one of the hands which has held me is placed directly over my heart. As I look into the eyes of the one who held my soul in his hands I know it is for the last time. At that point realisation of who the man is finally registers in my brain.

My smile is broad and my heart is full of such gratitude and love for this man I think it might explode all over again. God in his infinite wisdom did hear my suffering. HE sent one of his magnificent messengers to take away my pain and restore my fragmented heart.

selection of other lifetimes

(I): I have always known I inhabit an old soul. Accepting that singular aspect of me has never been a problem. It has enabled me to experience many lifetimes and many life lessons. Some lifetimes blessed me. Others did not. All are of my own choosing.

(II): It is inevitable that an air of impending doom hangs over my life as a raggedy pauper. That life deprives me of my adulthood. The dark and dank environment, and slum-fuelled conditions, starve my lungs of oxygen. Another type of starvation takes over my emaciated body and removes what little will to live I have remaining. I do not have long to wait. Along with so many unfortunates destined to experience similar existences, I die young.

(III): The extreme nature of a life surrounded by religious intolerance and fanatical forms of bigotry and ignorance is not just confined to the coastal village I find myself living in. It is endemic and is spreading rapidly across the length and breadth of the land. Everyone lives with the fear of being named and cast out. Neighbours turn against neighbours. The ones who suffer the most are the people who live on the margins of such intolerance. They are targeted for the harshest treatment. Many are hounded and persecuted for no good reason. If they fail to tell the supposed 'truth' they often have the 'truth' beaten out of them. It is not a good time to be living. This is borne out by the fact that another of my lives is so very nearly eclipsed. As a young woman I am placed in a 'ducking stool' and have to fight for my life as many in the over zealous partisan crowds bay for my death. I lose count of the number of times my body goes under the waves, yet still I cling on to my truth and refuse to hand over the life God has gifted me. To this day, I can still remember the taste of the seawater in my mouth and I hate the sensation of my head going under when I swim.

(IV): The clans draw me to the highlands of Scotland, but I know I am fighting a losing battle. My spirit deserts me. Sounds of blade clashing and sparking against blade, and the stench of rotting corporeal flesh, fills my nostrils and scars my mind with hideous images. The agonies of defeat hang over everything and I am destroyed from within. Every time I revisit Culloden Moor my heart remembers.

(V): The broad cuffs of golden filigree weigh heavily on my thin arms. I am a sickly child with an awkward gait, but a happy disposition. My condition is not a hindrance to me. The soft, royal blue

snake

Scarab
beetle

black scorpions

one of Godesses
pointed-eared cat

various spiders

fragments
of wood

webs

Olive branch

dried palm fronds

platters of dates

robes of my daily attire help to disguise my twisted torso. When I do happen to be ill, the curvature of my spine exacerbates the condition and sets my nerve endings alight. My physicians constantly marvel at my tolerance to withstand the pain. Everywhere I go, I am surrounded by the love of my family. I feel cherished and blessed. Further images of me as that young boy of royal descent during the reign of Nefertiti rush towards me. They bring back many memories of my charmed and privileged existence in the lands of the pharaohs.

(VI): Destiny has helped guide me towards the strong Egyptian connection part of memory. I have spent numerous lifetimes there. Flashbacks remind me of yet another life. Under the rule of a young, inexperienced pharaoh Egypt struggles. It is a time of great mystery and secrecy and subterfuge. People are wary. Many are plotting the downfall of the pharaoh, but I am not one of them. I am close to the half sister of the pharaoh, but not close enough to be considered a threat to the throne. My parents are blessed in having many children. I am the second eldest daughter. Choosing a name for me is straightforward. I am blessed with the same name as my mother, Sharika. Many people comment on my great beauty and learning, yet I know within myself I do not seek such compliments or the attention accompanying this. I accept the gifts bestowed on me but choose to disregard such vanity and follow a path committed to discipline and order.

Living in such uncertain times causes concern for women like me who make the decision not to marry. I am fortunate enough to have a protector to accompany me wherever I choose to go. My father insists upon this. I must comply and accept the protector he has provided. Marak is a man of considerable physical stature and keen intelligence. His ability to blend effortlessly into the background when necessary is one of his many talents. He is charged with watching over me and seeing I come to no harm. In the years since he came to me he has proven to be loyal and devoted to me. Every day, he accompanies me to the temple. As a priestess of the Sisterhood in the ancient mystery schools, I teach sacred geometry and languages of the ancestors. It is a rewarding life and I am revered by generations of students.

(VII): My duty is to tend to the needs of the pampered wives of noble heritage. In my hand, I am holding a fan. Made of ostrich feathers, the fan feels cumbersome. Sometimes I will stand for hours calming the wives with steady sweeps of the fan. Fevered brows are vanquished and the women are content once more. Not so, me. Much has been taken from me in this life, but I do not hand over everything so freely. My dignity is mine to own and remains intact. It comes as no surprise at all that my life as a eunuch holds scant memory for me.

(VIII): As a monk of a silent order, I walk along the stone arched walkway of the monastery. Many outside the order will see the spartan surroundings of the monastery and imagine the lives of the monks to be devoid of comfort. That is not true. Yes, the life is often hard, but when my brothers and I come together in unity it is enough to surpass any sense of deprivation we might be experiencing. The exposed position of the monastery means it lays itself open to winds from the north. Nature is fickle and unforgiving at times. On many occasions my extremities bear the brunt. It is a strange thing. I am often blue with cold, yet I feel no lasting hardship. During my time at the monastery I meet and connect with a member of my soul family. Every day, we walk together in silence. My heart is full of a life well lived.

I always acknowledge my lifetimes on earth as being completely separate from the energy work I currently carry out in angelic or otherworldly realms. They are two entirely different things. Although my mind is crammed full of lifetimes lived around the world, I have memory of only two lifetimes with any sort of meaningful spiritual connection. Recalling every detail is a little difficult, but this is the first of those two experiences.

(IX): I know I live in the Gobi desert and follow a spiritual pathway. On reflection, I think there is a portal of sorts nearby where angels come down from the heavens to earth to carry out their healings and blessings. I cannot confirm that, however. It is just a sense I have.

This particular lifetime rests in the not too distant past. Under the blistering heat of the open plains, I have my first visionary spiritual encounter. My life as a holy man amongst the nomadic herdsmen is harsh. I have no horse or sturdy yak to ease my burden, so I set out at first light to walk the miles to my brother and his wife. Looking around reminds me I still have some distance to travel. In every direction the landscape is barren and monotonous. No real identifiable features of any description exist to break the distant skyline. Deprived of rain, the soil beneath my feet has dried and crumbled to a fine powdery dust. There is no sign of life anywhere as I continue my solitary trek.

For some reason unknown to me at the time, my senses begin tuning into new vibrations, which suddenly spring up around me. Something is changing. The energy fields surrounding me take on alternative properties and dimensions. The earth I am standing on trembles slightly and I wonder if it is going to open up and swallow me. I am frightened now.

From out of nowhere a figure manifests. Bizarrely, everything is slowed down to a snail's pace. I know straight away that the emerging figure is that of a man. When he starts to rise up through the sprawling base of a deep mahogany coloured tree, he makes it seem like the most natural thing in the world. It is an extraordinary thing to see. Moments earlier the tree did not even exist.

Encountering something so surreal is a shock to my system and my hands start to sweat and shake. My forehead suddenly feels clammy and my stomach is churning. I wonder if I am going to be sick or pass out. Is this really happening to me? I begin to feel even more panicked and full of uncertainty. What am I supposed to do next? I am tempted to turn around and head back in the direction I have come, but something is pinning me to the spot and I cannot move a muscle.

Don't ask me how I know this, but when the figure turns to face me distant memory tumbles into place. I know straight away who he is. I recognise both the image in my head and the reality of the man in my line of vision. The figure is Archangel Gabriel. When he begins to speak his voice is soft and melodic. He says my name and calls me to him. As he opens his arms wide to embrace me, the fluid, glowing garments covering his lean frame fall gently to the ground. My fear disappears and I walk forward with unrestricted joy in my heart.

My one lasting memory of that day is the way his eyes draw me in. They are giant pools of magnetism and the colour of Burmese sapphires. The knowledge he passes onto me will end up being the cornerstone of my spiritual life. I do not think angels have souls like humans have souls, but somehow intuition tells me that my soul now rests within him. We are joined by the bonds of our calling.

(X): Memories of the long harsh winter and the tumultuous rising force of the cascading icy rivers of spring begin to fade. Summer is on its way. The time has come to follow the soft west wind and move to the fresh, sweet grasses where the buffalo can graze. Many moons have passed since my father gave me the name Morning Star. I am a young woman of the Sioux tribe, and being an only daughter I am my father's pride and joy. My heart swells with the love I feel for him and I am happy. That happiness extends to my tribal brothers and sisters and all who share my life. No boundaries exist when it comes to the love I have for my grandmother. She is very old and very wise, and instructs me in the ways of the Ancestors. From a very early age, she tells me the Ancestors are preparing me for something which will benefit all my people. It is not the first time I hear this said. Around the campfires at night I hear whispers that I am destined for something special in my life. I do not know what this thing is.

While the men set out with a small hunting party, and the children explore their favourite encampment, I am called by my mother to assist in setting up our new encampment. I go willingly. Responsibility for removing the hides and poles from the ponies and erecting the tepees always falls to the women. Every year, we follow the same routine. We leave the slightly higher ground and move to fresh pastures. We are always careful to place the tepees a little distance from the river, but not too far away for us to carry out our daily tasks. I love that I am following in the footsteps of my ancestors. It makes me smile knowing that generations of Sioux have lived here before me. It is a good time and place for all the families to be living. Food is abundant and the swallows are flying high.

Walking slowly towards the edges of the riverbank my heart soars as I catch sight of the brilliant, jewel-coloured dragonflies displaying and darting amongst the reeds and water grasses. They are astonishingly adept at flying and hovering and feeding on the wing. That is not the only thing which makes these remarkable insects stand out from other metamorphic nymphs. They are blessed with not one, but two sets of wings. This helps them fly fast and carry out incredible aerial feats. In gifting the dragonfly with both an air and water element, Mother Nature shows how benevolent she truly is.

The day is heady and filled with the smells of the long, sweet grasses and soft, flowering bushes. A few feet away, the river is calm. To those who know the river well, such calmness is often deceiving. It looks so still, yet underneath the surface small, brown, speckled trout battle against the flow and swim to the shallower waters up stream. My focus is distracted momentarily as the stillness of the day is pierced by an eagle plaintively calling out to its mate. The sound has a haunting, almost ethereal, quality to it and echoes for miles around. Every time I hear white throated messengers a shiver runs straight through me. A blanket of silence falls over everything. Birds nesting in the trees nearby hear the eagle's call and suddenly stop their trilling mid flow.

There is so much activity at the river edge it is difficult to choose what to look at next. My eyes latch onto the busy dipper setting about his business. For his size he is capable of catching a prodigious amount of larvae and water lice. He hops and jumps from stone to stone, filling his beak from the bounty of the river.

I continue to walk towards the bend where the river forks out in another direction. It is a favourite place of mine. Under the shade of a beautiful weeping silver birch, I often come to be on my own. I sit amongst the grasses and look up at Grandfather Sky above. We talk of many things and I feel blessed.

Finally, when I reach the bend and turn to approach 'my' tree, I am forced to stop in my tracks. I am astonished by what I see before me. Nothing is as I remember. I begin to get the strange sensation of walking into a dream, but it is a dream unlike any other I have encountered before. The birch tree stands where it always has, but its colouring has changed and its dimensions have increased ten fold. Beneath the low overhanging branches, carpets of white-winged butterflies flutter before coming to rest. It feels and looks as if the Ancestors have dipped brushes in extraordinary light of translucent profusion, and painted a canvas from the heavens. A voice in my head tells me not to be fearful and to go and sit under the tree. I listen to the voice and sit beneath the tree.

Everything I know about myself is placed to one side and another aspect of me fills my consciousness. In those few short minutes, my life changes forever. Outwardly, my physical make up appears the same to me, but something is going on inside me. It isn't just my thoughts. My heart picks up its beat. I sense it expand and fill with Light. The Light slowly spreads from my heart and reaches the rest of my body. Words cannot really explain what it feels like when my body adapts, and my entire physical being becomes that very same Light. In the past, elders of the tribe spoke of such things, but I could never imagine I could have such an experience. I am no longer filled with doubt. The reality of my life is what it is. Accepting this incredible gift of Light comes easily.

I know I must wait and am content to do so. Thoughts of my life and my family briefly toy with my memory before they fade and float away. There is something otherworldly about the events unfolding, yet I know I am grounded to the earthly plain. My breath catches in my throat as I see a magnificent white wolf coming towards me. He is not alone. Other animals follow in his broad, padded wake. When the bear materialises out of thin air, a trickle of unease settles upon me. Never ever in my life have I seen a bear so large or with such a sense of presence. Head up, sniffing the air, it walks through the grasses at a gentle pace. Next to come into view is the agile and powerfully limbed mountain lion. As he moves, he flicks his tail from side to side. In quick succession, the lion makes way for an eagle and a snake. The snake is the length of a tall, young sapling.

The coats and skins of the animals are the purest and whitest of white. Although they are all wild creatures, somehow I sense they would not be averse to human touch. I smile to myself. Am I really giving consideration to such a crazy notion? Tempting as it is, caution steps in and redirects my thoughts. All the animals come to stand in front of me. I hold their gaze for several minutes. It is at this point that some higher spiritual aspect of self washes over me. Finally freed from the last strictures placed around it, I end up revealing my heart to them.

I am conscious of time merging and acknowledging my Truth. A short while later all eye contact stops. The animals move off and come to sit at my side.

There is no time to think. Ancestors come from the four directions and make their way towards me. Their power and incredible energy reaches me before they do. I sit quietly, trying to absorb as much of those qualities as I can. Inner knowing informs me the Ancestors are here to impart knowledge and wisdom and pay homage to me. Is the prophecy of the Ancestors about to come true? Have they something special in mind for me and my tribe? I am at a loss for words. The honour they afford me reveals much about my forefathers and the faith they have in me. Why am I chosen? Am I really worthy of such an honour?

Along with the animals, the Ancestors form a circle around the tree and around me. They stand quietly watching me. All are sensing the vulnerability and incomprehension as I am overcome with powerful emotions. I wish my grandmother was here to comfort me. She would know what to do. As my tears of humility flow freely down my face, I still do not fully understand what if anything is expected of me.

I need not worry so much. The Ancestors and the animals are here to help me through the mountain of questions inside my head. I give myself over to them.

The compulsion to close my eyes is strong and I concede. Time passes without me acknowledging its length. My mind is suffused with images and words and ancient knowledge. There is a purity of Spirit in everything I do, and in everything I now know. I am changed beyond all recognition inside. It feels as extraordinary as it is. Every ounce of my being rejoices and gives thanks to the part the Ancestors and the animals have played in my life. I realise our parting is imminent. The time has come for the final part of my experience. I am ready.

The circle parts and I can see the river once more. A little way off, an outline appears. It is the figure of a young woman, not unlike me. She is surrounded by light, and I cannot yet see her face clearly. Her clothing is made from the softest white deer skins and the moccasins supporting her feet are covered in delicate turquoise beads. A hush is falling over everything. Even the air I breathe is held in suspended motion.

The young woman is standing before me now. I can see her beautiful face framed by hair the colour of polished onyx. Her energy is unique to her. She has a generous giving spirit, and I feel her gift surge through me, filling me with even more ancient knowledge and Light. On top of everything else I am experiencing today this feels like completion. Then I realise it is. I am instantly aware that part of me resides in her and her in me. We are two parts of the whole finally coming together. She reaches out and takes hold of my hand and straight away I know what I am to do. In order to bring unity to my tribe and all the other tribes I must go with her now and leave my old life behind. Times of conflict are to remain in the past. It is over. A new Nation of Tribes is to be created. The Ancestors have written that this creation of a Nation is what I must do. It is up to me to walk forward and create my own footsteps and fulfil my destiny.

Extract no. 6:
The departure

The long, lazy nights of summer had faded, confined only to memory. All too soon it seemed those languorous days of idleness gave way to the burnished days of autumn...my favourite season of all. I had been living with the knowledge for the best part of three months. Whilst I understood why I had taken the steps I had, it did not pacify my fluctuating emotions, or the realisation of abandoning something precious in my life. One day I was happy, the next day left me feeling mournful. Doubt reared its head then just as quickly it departed again. Time moved forward. Each step taken felt like a threat to erode any sense of equilibrium within me. There was nothing I could have done to make events any easier. I had completed the work intended for me and chosen the path in which my future destiny lay. There could be no going back. My energies were needed elsewhere.

As the day of departure grew closer, the sense of loss had firmly embedded and rooted itself deep within my psyche. When I had made the decision to move away from my home of fifteen years to pastures new, I knew the day I said farewell to my own little piece of heaven on earth would be a difficult one. During the build up to my departure I had been wracked with feelings of guilt and lingering bouts of nostalgia. Had I done the right thing? I could not deny the compelling thoughts that had driven me and the whole process along. There were certainly times when I struggled to come to terms with my decision making. Why had I so suddenly, and without any definitive reasoning or creditable justification, arrived at that decision? My head acknowledged it was the right and only thing to do, but my heart failed to recognise that and, as a result, it felt the pain. Both my daughters thought I was completely mad to even contemplate moving. They loved our home. I did experience enormous pangs of regret, but the reality of the situation was there would be no backing out; contracts had been exchanged, commitments had been made. The documentation had been finalised and was legally binding. My beautiful property found itself on the cusp of welcoming its new guardians. It was time for me to move on and lay down new foundations for my memory bank.

The day dawned, but it was not an easy dawning. Familiar delicate pink shards and expansive tracks of striated golden hues, normally patterning the ragged skyline with such wondrous grace, were making a statement by absenting themselves. Torrential rain lashed against the windows. I could see solid jets of water spewing outwards, tripping and tumbling over the debris-laden roans, splattering and directing the overflow onto the paving below. The wind was relentless and savage, battering and bruising the century-old lime and elm trees encircling and protecting the wild garden to the west. Normally, the sturdy bushes and shrubbery were sheltered from the elements. Against such ferocious odds their valiant struggles were proving futile. Nature held her ground and stood firm as established roots threatened to dislodge themselves from the loose, sodden soil. Such a powerful and sustained aerial bombardment would inevitably result in plants with a tenuous hold being ripped from their earthly dominion. It wasn't easy watching such decimation.

As I peered out of the bedroom windows that overlooked the orchard and old walled garden, the child in me resurfaced and the temptation proved too much. I deliberately allowed my breath to make contact with the object it so obviously desired. For those few short seconds a living mist of exhalation created its own unique memory by enveloping the small, thinning panes of glass before evaporating into a vacuous maze of nothingness.

From the security of my vantage point I could see and hear the power of the storm. It was wreaking havoc with every living thing in the garden. The crab apple and damson trees, which only days earlier had revelled in their glorious autumn mantle, began to look vulnerable and naked. Wind tore through their gnarled branches, whipping up discarded leaves, scattering and depositing skeletal foliage onto the pond and lichen encrusted stonework of the garden seat. It seemed an abrupt and particularly callous ending to the bearers of such a bountiful harvest. I knew these trees well and I had loved their bold statement beauty. They were still beautiful in my mind. I knew once the storm abated and the trees acclimatised themselves to their nakedness they would take on another, less resplendent but equally captivating, cloak of beauty.

Everywhere I looked that day memories and sounds came rushing back. It was not just the gardens or surrounding countryside which triggered instant flashbacks. Pictures of my beloved mother, feet barely touching the floor, head tilting gently forward as she reluctantly succumbed to her afternoon nap in her favourite oak armchair in the kitchen began to emerge. It had always been my armchair by the fire but since its refurbishment the chair came under careful and renewed scrutiny from my mother. Without anything actually being said, I knew she found the comfortably constructed proportions and attractive new coverings of the chair to her liking. Before I could reclaim rightful ownership, the chair showed its fickleness by transferring its allegiance. From that moment on it became forever known as granny's chair. I did not mind in the least. It suited the countenance of my mother so very much more.

When I originally moved into the manse the kitchen very quickly established itself as the hub and epicentre of anything and everything. Part of the attraction was its natural ability to draw people in and make anyone feel welcome. It was within this nurturing environment that many of my very last memories of my mother were created. I can still hear the sound and intonations of her voice. First it would rise then it would dip in a lyrical, sing-song fashion. As was often the case, if something amused her then invariably laughter would follow. For someone so short-changed in the height stakes, she had a resounding and highly infectious laugh. Never a day would pass without the two of us attempting to put our fractured society or the ailments of the world to rights. When we were not doing that there was always a story to tell or retell, ensuring passage into the annals of our family life. Both of us could always find something or other to chatter about and wile away the hours. We never ran out of things to say or share with one another, and would spend endless hours in deep, and occasionally not so deep, conversation. We enjoyed the company of one another and respected each other's opinions, no matter how diverse they might have been.

Whenever I look back and think of either of my parents I know how inordinately blessed I was in my relationship with both of them. Whilst I was always extremely close to my father, sadly he plays only a small part in this particular extract from my journal. After his death, the grief and very real sense of loss resulted in my mother and I becoming even closer than before. Whilst I could never even partly fill the void left by my father's passing, I hope I was in some way able to bring my mother comfort and ease the torment in her heart.

When I think of my mother it is always with wonderment and enormous pride at the way she overcame so much in her own life. She was an extraordinary woman. Along with so many of her generation, she had lived through defining passages in history. Although she had not come out of those passages unscathed, she had been more fortunate than others and had lived to tell her tale. She always saw life as a wondrous and special gift. It was to be embraced and lived to the full. Without wishing to sanctify her in any way, those who knew her well found her a source of great inspiration. No one doubted her selflessness or giving nature. The love she always found time to express towards her family is remembered every single day of every single year.

My thoughts return to other memorable chapters of my time living in the manse. Just a few years ago, in the morning room directly beneath my feet, my eldest daughter and her fiancée had exchanged their words of betrothal and the promise of a future life together. My daughter had always declared if she were ever to marry it would not be a traditional type of wedding. She was not one for fuss and, in her own words, nor was she a fluffy, meringue dress type of a girl. She preferred something less formal. So it proved to be. She decided to break with tradition and have a best man. His name was John. He was fantastically humorous and I understood straight away why my daughter had chosen him as her best man. I still smile when I think of him. When the actual exchanging of vows took place only very close family were present. Other guests would arrive after the service. John had obviously decided the bride did not have sole and exclusive rights when it came to making a grand entrance. It was incumbent upon him to make an entrance of his own. Kitted out, somewhat incongruously, in a suit of Ancient Buchanan tartan, he stood expectantly at the bottom of the stairs, guitar at the ready. I could see from the expression on his face that he was definitely nervous. As my beautiful daughter gracefully descended the sweeping staircase he serenaded her with a song from West Side Story. The sweet clear sound of his voice and the sheer beauty of the moment guaranteed there was not a dry eye in the house.

It was only later we realised that while the short, late afternoon service was taking place inside the house, wonderful things were also taking place outside. An acquaintance happened to be driving past at the time, and she had seen dozens of wild collared doves circling round and around the house. Several pairs of doves normally inhabited the walled garden, but certainly not dozens of them. Were the majority of the doves in the vicinity somehow attracted and drawn towards the special energy surrounding that specific moment in the day? Who knows? When the guests started arriving many commented on the delicate white feathers strewn across the wide stone steps of the pillared sandstone portico. The spiritual connection between birds and angels is a strong one. Were the feathers that day bird feathers or angel feathers? Each of us must make up our own minds as to that.

The house acted almost like a guardian at times, and held onto so many special moments from all our lives. Who could forget the countless days of laughter and glorious summers with the girls and their wonderful groups of friends, or the girlie, hen weekend of my youngest daughter when too much champagne was consumed and lots of silly games were played? The memories flooded my senses. They were so numerous and so vivid they threatened to engulf me. What to pick out of such a golden treasure chest of love and familial remembrances?

Christmas and the accompanying festivities were particularly happy times for us as a family. The build up to Christmas was always the most exciting. The cake, which had been left waiting in splendid isolation for the best part of two months, finally received its luxurious coating of marzipan and glossy, thick, white icing. Bedraggled, hand-stitched remnants of advent were resurrected and hung as childhood reminders in each of the girls' bedrooms. Everything gradually started to come together. The house would be decked out with large sprays of plump-berried holly, interspersed with old foraged pine cones and lavish, glistening garlands of yew and flowering ivy. All the activity seemed to make the house come even more alive than ever before. The large drawing room fast became the star attraction. We all tended to gravitate towards the brightest jewel in the festive crown. Standing directly in front of the large bay window overlooking the garden was the most beautiful vision of the entire Christmas season. At almost ten feet high and overburdened with lights and glitter and a profusion of twinkling, coloured glass balls, the tree flashed and sparkled. A huge array of gifts would nestle silently beneath the lower branches of fresh smelling pine, each mesmerising and teasing with promises of untold pleasure. Who amongst us has not revelled at some time or another in the experience of at first patiently untying the carefully placed ribbon then, when that proved to be too much of a hindrance and irritation, almost savagely ripping apart the gift wrapping until finally the glorious gift reveals itself? What joy, as for the very first time, the eyes catch a glimpse of the gift. After the euphoria, a minuscule sense of regret flits around the periphery. Having been crafted and sculpted with so much love and attention to detail, the shredded wrappings would lay discarded and abandoned, waiting for their rather inglorious ending. Christmas was a time of great celebration. The house would expand and somehow manage to accommodate all. Everyone would congregate and come together to share in the joy of being a family.

Such a truly special home and events created their own unique memories. As I reflected, I could quite honestly state that I felt happy and privileged to have been able to share a small part of my time on earth in such a sacred and blessed environment. To have been privy to the energies and secrets of the house and the gardens was something I would take with me no matter where I was in the world. I would cherish them always.

to glimpse. . .perchance to dream

When I first set eyes upon the old manse house, secreted away off the rutted farm track, I remember thinking how sad it looked and how very dark it must have been to actually live in the house. Dense vegetation and unruly shrubbery smothered the area to the front of the property. Heavy, half-closed wooden shutters on the upper windows acted as deterrents to any form of natural daylight. It was probably wrong of me to give energy to the totally unfounded notions I had of the inhabitants living in the manse. I found it almost impossible to imagine the current occupants being anything other than depressed by the lack of light in their daily living. Instant judgement on any given situation without the correct facts in place can often lead to misguided preconceptions. Perhaps the house was not as negatively impacted as I had supposed? Nonetheless, it was hard to shake off the air of solemnity the property projected.

In all the time I had lived in the village I had never seen anyone either enter or leave the property. That in itself was a little unusual. I must admit I found the whole property and its reclusive occupancy scenario somewhat curious and intriguing. Questions seeking answers quickly lodged and took up residency. Frustratingly for me, the majority of the questions remained unanswered. Undaunted by the lack of information, I resolved to keep my interest in the property and its occupants alive. With no one to bounce my theories off, I resorted to one-way conversations with myself. Whilst this internal dialoguing was taking place, in another part of my brain something else was occurring. I was consciously aware of a shift taking place within me. As soon as the property came under more focused and detailed scrutiny from me, I began to sense a strange, almost compulsive, magnetism being projected from the property. It was definitely grabbing hold of my attention and sucking me in. I had to ask myself if I really wanted that to happen. The answer to the question posed was a resounding yes. Having questioned for so long, I decided to listen to what my own intuition was telling me. Accepting this still didn't stop me, or some of my more fanciful notions, from slipping into the thought process.

For the shortest period of time, my thoughts ventured into fantasy territory allowing me free rein to imaginings about the property and its invisible owners which were absurd in their silliness. On one occasion, I remember some of my more whimsical thoughts become actual fictional representations one might imagine gracing the pages of The Grimm Brothers fairy tales. That really appealed to my sensibilities at the time and amused the inner child within. I began to wonder what sort of persons lived within the confines of so grey and foreboding a structure? Did they secrete themselves away on purpose, and if they did, then why? Were they so very different? Was something making them too afraid to show their faces in public?

Without too much encouragement, my mind went into overdrive and rather bizarrely conjured up images of strange elusive figures with large carbuncles on their noses and warts covering their ears. Those thoughts rapidly progressed to the possibility of cavernous, hidden-from-view dungeons, deep inside the bowels of the property. Did all the local warlocks and witches converge there at night in rooms fuelled by flickering candlelight? After that, it wasn't too great a leap to imagine goblins and otherworldly creatures. I smiled to myself as a thought crossed my mind. If I actually plucked up the courage to walk right up and knock on the main door of the property would I somehow be spirited away, never to be seen again? Would any one person even notice my disappearance in time to do something about saving me?

Whilst I registered the humour in my musings, I did not give such fleeting mind imagery any reason to become permanent fixtures. No matter how tempting they might have been, the fantasy-fuelled wonderings faced relegation and eventual banishment.

Through the village grapevine I established that my fanciful notions on the habitation of the manse were just that. The manse had full time occupants. They actively participated in village life and contributed considerably to the enrichment of the local community. How could I have thought otherwise?

Most mornings would see both myself and the family spaniel set out for a lengthy walk along the sheltered shoreline of the bay and onto the coastal pathway beyond. Every afternoon, unless the weather was too miserable, we would set off again for a second, less vigorous, walk of the day. This would inevitably lead us up the country track and past the manse. It did not take long for subtle changes in the daily patterning to begin emerging. Without knowing why, or indeed if it would ever become a reality, I began to indulge myself with thoughts of one day living in the house. Before I knew where I was, the thought went from being a small kernel of an idea into a full-blown desire. I could visualise it all so clearly. In my head at least, I was already there.

Sadly, a family tragedy within the manse became the deciding factor on its future. Although circumstances had conspired to create an opportunity for me to realise my desire, that opportunity was as a result of another family and their grief. It was not how I had envisaged events unfolding.

I had always recognised the house's enormous potential. Quite undaunted, I committed myself to the purchase of the property and everything that entailed. So, the metamorphosis began. With a great deal of gentle persuasion, and a healthy injection of commitment and time, the outwardly soulless property began its journey of rediscovering its hidden qualities. In a relatively short period of time, the house fulfilled its true promise and turned into a beautiful and vibrant home full of light and colour. Life and energy were restored to the elegant Georgian proportions. The transformation, whilst arduous, brought the house almost full circle to final completion.

The gardens were an altogether more challenging prospect. There were three in total. Each had its own unique set of challenges. The front was south facing and completely overgrown. It was choked with mountainous piles of rubble and weeds and awkward invitational stones which would almost certainly guarantee injuries to life and limb. Heavy-duty machinery would be needed to bulldoze a pathway to the front door. The wild garden was west facing, and again choked almost to within an inch of its life with overgrown shrubbery and wild scrambling brambles. Crumbling, rotting branches and wide-jagged stumps of heavily infested elms lay silently in the long grasses waiting for the unsuspecting. The walled garden which faced south east would definitely be the most problematical. Someone had attempted to try and keep things under some sort of control, but the futility of such effort was all too apparent. They had been fighting a losing battle. There were little pockets of real beauty within the ancient walls, but they were too few and certainly far between. To undertake restorative projects of such magnitude would be nothing short of staggering.

I predicted that resurrecting the gardens would turn out to be a true labour of love. The prediction was accurate. It took years to establish any semblance of order or shape into the dilapidated horticultural wilderness. The rewards were well worth the endeavour. Every inch weeded every branch pruned every living plant nurtured and coaxed to face the sun revelled once more in self-regeneration and glorious growth. Areas where the struggle for survival had been the greatest were touched by a minor miracle and transformed into havens of great beauty and tranquillity. There was a tangible living energy in all three gardens. I could always sense it, but could not always define it. The whole family loved the gardens. The walled garden seemed to hold a particular fascination, not only for the family but for the birds and wildlife which inhabited it.

Autumn was always my favourite season. On that I never really wavered. I readily admit there were numerous occasions whilst living at the manse, immersed in the gifts of Mother Nature, when I could have so easily been persuaded otherwise. When in May every year the bluebells came through in the wild and walled gardens I was amazed how utterly breathtaking and entrancing the gardens became. A living, breathing canvas of perfumed motion brushed with a palette of subtle blues and the softest pastel pinks. This display of nodding profusion lasted well into the month of June and faded, just as other floral delights began to unfurl and come into full bloom. There was always a plant in bud or about to bud somewhere or another in the gardens. That was the way the planting continued throughout all the seasons.

My thoughts eased me gently and effortlessly back to summertime, which was always the most active and productive time of the year. I found it nigh on impossible to select a favourite event from a plethora of sun-fuelled memories. Instead, I decided to let memories surface without any directional input or guidance from me. The response was immediate as images flooded my mind. Once seen, who could forget the majesty of the hovering peacock butterflies with their glorious markings, or the brief flashing brilliance of the damselflies as they darted across the lily pads on the surface of the pond? Throughout the long, warm days swallows in residence would swoop in low at impossible angles, skimming water from the very same pond. Later on in the season, the orchard would play host to carpets of red admirals feasting on the nectar and sweet harvest of the fallen fruits. I remember the year the hen pheasant decided to nest at the centre of a massive old gooseberry bush in the wild garden. For months I had been watching her feign indifference towards the handsome cock pheasant as he preened and strutted with assured arrogance and sovereignty. The daily ritual started early, with the cock taking every available opportunity to 'display' his splendid copper plumage and flash his vibrant crimson throat feathers. His attempts were not in vain.

The hen disappeared for a short duration and I did begin to wonder if something had happened to her. I need not have worried. For very good reason her attention had been focused elsewhere. Out of sight of any would be predators she had guarded her eggs well. Thirteen chicks hatched within days of each other. Mercifully, the rooks and crows nesting nearby did not have to resort to their usual ruthless, cannibalistic tendencies and that season at least left the chicks well alone. As the delicious dessert gooseberries grew plumper, so did the chicks. When mama first took her offspring walkabout they had not yet developed their flight feathers. They were too young to even attempt the flight over the garden wall, but skinny enough to squeeze under the buckled wooden structure of the ancient looking gate. Every morning, the chicks would emerge from the safety of the nest and scurry through the wild garden grasses trying their hardest to keep up with the hen as she set about her daily constitutional around the gardens. It was one of the most delightful and comical events of the day watching the pheasant parade. As day passed into early evening, and the scraping and foraging ceased, the entire entourage would regroup and make tracks again towards the safety of the gooseberry bush. Amazingly, when the time came to fly the nest eleven of the chicks had succeeded in making it through the first fraught-with-danger months. The hen must have felt safe for she survived the rigours of the shooting season and returned to rear more chicks the following year.

The second summer in my new home was a time of rediscovering and reawakening on a spiritual level. Not only had I made giant inroads into my plans for the restoration of the house, but I had also become aware that I was not alone in my quest to bring the heartbeat back into the gardens. For the longest time, I had sensed several energies inhabiting the outside space. They made no attempt to conceal their energy from me. Each adjusted to a new energy and presence on their patch. I was aware from an early stage of a single energy in particular standing out from the rest. It would tease from a distance without revealing very much about itself. I knew by the way the energy observed and absorbed every little detail I undertook that remaining apart from each other's energy field was not a viable option. All I felt that was needed was acceptance on both our sides.

As the scales of balance sought to take root and advance, neglected areas of garden caught their first real glimpse of sunlight in years. What a magical time it was. Though still showing a degree of hesitancy to completely reveal its true identity, the reluctant energy did seem to approve of my efforts to revitalise the garden. Coming under such scrutiny did not disturb me in any way. It was the complete opposite. I found the presence of such energy comforting. The longer the observations continued, the stronger the feeling became that the energy was waiting for me to take the initiative and instigate a 'proper' meeting between the two of us. It was important to me that the energy knew I was a safe pair of hands and it could trust me. Before that could happen I knew both of us would have to be patient just a little longer. Timing was everything.

Days and weeks merged into each other. When the weather permitted, I would manoeuvre my wheelchair over and around the pitted obstacle course which at that time represented a pathway. Sometimes, I would come seriously unstuck and have to find novel ways of extricating myself from impossible situations. On more than one occasion upon hearing me call out for assistance, my kindly neighbours, Ben and Florence, would come to my rescue. For the most part, determination to advance proved the victor. I would not give in easily. With almost maniacal fervour I would singlehandedly wend my way across fragmented brickwork and through a seemingly impenetrable concoction of long, twisting grasses and mountains of sticky-burrs. In time, reminders of dereliction were eventually brushed aside and new passageways created.

It was inevitable that progress would bring about change, and I was happy about that. I was often conscious of my solitary status living at the manse, yet I never felt alone. As I got to know the gardens a little better I found myself stopping for no particular reason at certain spots. At other spots I would get a very real sense of friendly yet silent energies accompanying me. I started the gradual process of rekindling an ancient friendship by reconnecting with Mother Earth and the spirits of nature. It was a wonderful time knowing that everything was slowly starting to come together.

It was another clear and sunny day, so we made the decision to make the most of it and go out into the walled garden. Picnic blankets were carefully positioned then everyone stretched out on the moss-cushioned grass determined to enjoy the afternoon rays. It was in this setting amidst the chatter of a few fellow light workers that my erstwhile guardian decided the moment of definitive reveal was nigh. At first I thought it might be a trick of light as the hazy, almost irregular, outline appeared across the wide uneven expanse of lawn by the far away wall. The more I studied the shape, the more convinced I became of the existence of a figure. As if to satisfy any niggling doubts I might have had, the figure chose to step forward into full view. A frisson or spark of recognition shot through me. Straight away, I felt the connection between us.

The figure was dressed like a monk in loose, flowing garb with a faded and frayed rope twisting its way around his capacious girth. With a bald, domed head he looked as though he had just stepped through time after a day working in the fields nearby. As I continued to study the figure I could literally feel time coming to a complete standstill. I was conscious of only one thing and that was the way the monk's eyes sought out mine, drawing me in. All the noise and motion around me faded away. Even the birds were silent. I tried concentrating on what my eyes were seeing. There was a great deal to try and assimilate. My mind had to adapt quickly and register the actuality of this new unfolding reality. I remember quite clearly the sensation of butterflies doing somersaults and a spot of freefalling in my stomach. This giddying feeling was accompanied by the strong desire to go straight over to the spot the monk was standing on. Everything had a real sense of immediacy and urgency about it, but it was an immediacy tinged with a certain degree of caution. I hesitated for only a few seconds. In the process I learnt something about myself. When it came right down to it that first step was a step too far. Somewhere between the internal verbal confusion of 'do it, don't do it' I persuaded myself not to immediately react and reveal the presence of the monk. I suppose something inside me didn't want to attract too much attention to what was actually happening to me. There was another aspect to this that had me wondering. Was I the only one to notice the monk? Were others having a similar experience? In my confusion, I suppose I faltered a little. It was only afterwards I could truthfully admit to myself that I was probably a little scared. As I reflected on the unique opportunity I had been afforded I realised something important. Although I had been blessed with the opportunity to connect with the monk, I had not felt secure enough in my own abilities to take hold of that opportunity. Suddenly, everything changed. In the blinking of an eye my newly found guardian was gone.

It was ridiculous to feel so cheated and bereft, but at the time those were exactly the extreme emotions I experienced. I was annoyed with myself and the lack of faith I had shown. Normally, I felt comfortable in my own ability to work alongside energies. I knew my strengths and my weaknesses, and never presumed to take any introductory energy for granted. What had happened? Why hadn't I just been brave enough and taken that initial step and gone right over to where the figure was standing?

The rest of the day passed in conversation and laughter and good-hearted camaraderie. It had been almost impossible to concentrate on what others were saying. My mind was elsewhere occupied with tantalising thoughts of the monk and the energy surrounding him. I treasure all my friends and I love when they visit, but from the moment the monk made his appearance I was desperate to be alone with my thoughts. Eventually, my wish was granted and my friends departed. I was finally on my own and able to explore without interruption the events of the afternoon.

The next couple of days were both exciting and frustrating in equal measure. Whilst I had longed to get out into the garden again, I had to content myself with being confined indoors. Much needed rain had deluged the surrounding countryside, topping up the water table once more and rejuvenating the parched soil. Everything in the gardens looked quenched and vibrant and full of life.

My chair almost flew down the steel structure of the ramp and onto the path leading to the walled garden. It was time for me to seek out my companion monk and reaffirm he was not just a figment of my imagination. I felt the first tiny tendrils of doubt creep in and gently take hold. Would he appear again or wouldn't he? In my heart I knew what the outcome would be. He did not disappoint. Almost on cue, he materialised in the exact same spot I had first laid eyes upon him. At first glance his stance seemed slightly stooped, almost wearied, as though he had been waiting for this moment for a very long time. Standing stock still, he stared right at me studying my reaction, waiting for acknowledgement and recognition. I could feel my heart constrict then expand. Its rhythm went awry, rapidly increasing then decreasing in tempo. The moment I tried relaxing into my breath my concentration shifted and everything stilled. I became aware of the Light. There was nothing else. It became the key element in sustaining the continuance of life itself. Slowly it filtered through to the centre of all that was me. Nothing could halt the steady flow of Light filling me from within. It was extraordinary to experience a blessing such as that. No word or dialogue was needed. Sure in the knowledge and acceptance of our kindred connection, the monk and I smiled at each other.

The distance separating us was only a matter of ten or twelve feet or so, yet it was close enough for me to clearly see his large gnarled hands and the darkened lines of earth beneath his squared off fingernails. He wore identical garments to those that had first alerted me to his presence. Closer inspection revealed them to be functional enough for the seasonal task at hand. Made of a coarse hemp sacking, the garments seemed very basic. I found myself thinking that they certainly would not have stood up well to colder, more vigorous weather. How silly and illogical a thought was that? Leaning against a long wooden implement, which looked like a cross between a hoe and a peat cutter, I noticed the posture of the monk relax. My eyes drifted down towards his feet for the first time. Although I probably should have expected to see what I did, it nonetheless came as a bit of a shock to realise that, apart from a smattering of loose soil particles, his feet were entirely bare.

Looking back at that time it still intrigues me how easily and readily I accepted the existence of the monk. That was the way it was meant to be, and that was the way it was. I felt no real overriding need to ply my companion monk with a barrage of endless questioning. It was not something that I recall as being uppermost in my mind, nor did it seem a pressing priority. What would I have asked him that would have made a difference and enriched the experience further? The silence we shared sat comfortably with me. I was perfectly content to be in the moment without distractions of an inquisitorial mind. Others might think my actions odd, but I really just wanted to enjoy the space of the garden with my monk.

After that initial wordless meeting it did not take long for communication to stake its claim. My monk's name was Magnus. What truly astounded me was his admission that he had been in and around the area since medieval times, working the fields and tilling the land. When you hear something like that you can accept or choose not to accept. There were no doubts at all in my mind and I chose acceptance. I cannot recall all our conversations, or exactly what was said, but generally Magnus and I spoke of the gardens encircling the manse. The present walled garden had only been in existence for one hundred and seventy years but Magnus had always loved it. Even through the neglected years he had always known that someone would come along one day and breathe life back into it. Whatever the reason, the universe had worked its magic to ensure that person would be me.

Every step and every turn I made in the gardens over my guardianship of them I sensed the presence of Magnus. I might not always have seen him, but I knew he was there. Sometimes days would pass without a sighting of him then, when I least expected it, he would make an appearance and accompany me. As we wound our way around the garden we might or might not talk. More often than not we would share telepathically. It was during these times I spent with Magnus that I began to uncover forgotten strengths and a renewed sense of my own spirituality.

Usually when Magnus and I met up it would be at his favourite spot in the garden. To this day I can still visualise him standing beside the vigorous golden ivy on the west wall. Sheltered to the front by old varieties of fragrant Gallica roses and pink flowering sage, he would wait. To the right of him, struggling through low-lying ground plants, was a glorious straggly clump of vibrant forget-me-not. As far as I was concerned never was a flower more aptly named; tiny in dimension, yet gifts of absolute perfection. Right throughout my life I have always associated forget-me-not with angels and angelic energy. Moments before the energies reveal themselves, images of these exquisite little flowers will appear. It is always a special moment. So it always was with Magnus.

Over my tenure-ship of the manse there were other secrets to discover about this special place I called home. As work progressed on the wild and front gardens, further energies came out of hiding and revealed themselves. They would tease me as I sat at the dining room window looking out over the fields beyond. 'Tree Man' and 'Himself' inhabited the two magnificent lime trees by the front gates of the property. They became the gatekeepers and protectors of all things growing and living within their realms. Two other colourful characters of no known name also inhabiting the grounds rapidly appropriated new names and were thereafter known as Napoleon and Happy Jack. Seldom together, they loved to meander around the gardens, walking amongst the trees and carpets of wild flowers. Occasionally, the slim ethereal figure of a nature spirit would gracefully glide into view to accompany them. Of great disappointment to me was the fact that she always managed to conceal her features. Never once did she grant me the rare privilege of being able see her face. I contented myself with the knowledge of just how blessed I had been to see her at all.

Only towards the end of my time at the manse did a beautiful tree sprite make itself known. Although extraordinarily elusive, when she did decide to make an appearance she was not exactly shy and retiring. This was a sprite who loved lots of glitter and sparkle and wasn't afraid to show it off! One might have expected her to be a study in nature's green, but that was not the case. Her wings were iridescent wonders, and her clothing the most beautiful shade of palest blue. In the blinking of an eye she would swiftly dart from branch to flower before disappearing into the dense foliage once more. I loved catching glimpses of her, but sometimes months would pass before she 'showed up' again.

I know I was extremely blessed and privileged to have the opportunity of experiencing living in that particular place and at that particular time of my life. It was extraordinary. I recognise how unbelievably fortunate I was when Spirit gifted me with sightings of Mother Nature's sprites and other elementals. Although little recollection remains of words having been spoken, there nonetheless existed an understanding, an intuitive knowing and coming together of something very special.

To this day, I miss my special home. Whilst my heart and thoughts might on occasion linger over the memories, I am reconciled that the house and gardens are in the safe keeping of other custodians. As I reach the end of my writings of those days, I cannot complete without one final mention. The one thing I miss above all else from that time in my life is the companionable presence of Magnus. The way his gentle, generous spirit chose to share is something that will live on in my heart forever.

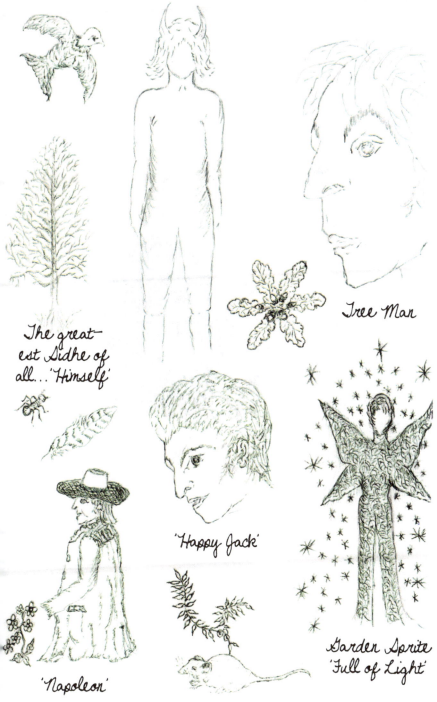

The great-
est Sidhe of
all... 'Himself'

Tree Man

'Happy Jack'

'Napoleon'

Garden Sprite
'Full of Light'

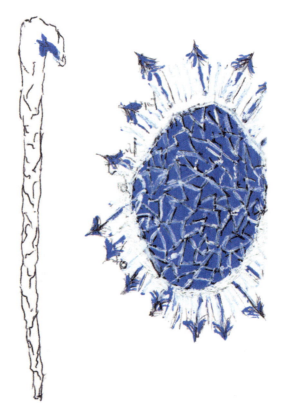

Extract no. 7: The Oberon staff (a brief introduction)

There is little or no effort involved in resurrecting times that have left indelible marks and lasting impressions upon my life. Writing this down is as cathartic as I knew it would be and triggers a whole host of remembrances and emotions. As the gentle road of reflection is teased into forward motion, once more the memories come rushing back. Even with the passage of time, I still have physical and mental recall of the days leading up to my first gift from Spirit. The reason I remember those days so well is because they were so normal. If things had been off balance or out of sync in any way I would have noticed. I had no concerns about everything being exactly the way it should.

Just as the daylight hours had navigated their familiar path, so they rapidly faded and gave way to the inky, star-strewn mistiness of the night skies. There was no indication or any sense at all of a major event about to take place. My adept internal radar receptors were not picking up on any signals, imaginary or otherwise. Nothing would have led me to suppose that this somewhat calm and relaxed state of affairs was about to change, yet change it did. The knock-on effect would prove to be thought provoking, and lead to the advancement and inner knowing of me.

I had no fore-knowledge that a gift of great spiritual significance to me was quite literally laying waiting in the wings. As I delve back into distant recall, I don't think I was aware enough at that time to realise that celestial gifts and physical representations of form, other than angelic, were even a possibility. When Spirit stepped forward and presented me with a Staff of life-size proportions I was stunned and almost disbelieving. Because nothing like this had ever happened to me before I couldn't quite get my head around it. It would take time, and an inordinate amount of patience, to fully unravel the events of the evening.

I didn't know then that this was just the very beginning of something far more evolved and spiritually challenging than anything I had previously experienced. The participation of Spirit didn't stop at the gift of a solitary Staff, but turned out to be even more complex and munificent than I could ever have envisaged. To receive one Staff was in itself incredible enough, but when I realised over a period of a few short months that I was to be the recipient of four separate Staffs it was nothing short of astounding. I knew immediately that the appearance of the Staffs in this period of my life was no coincidence. These events would be life changing, and would become key factors and vital elements in my rapid progression towards a more awakened state of spiritual awareness.

Before the story of how the Staffs came into my everyday life can be told, however, I must first of all tell you about certain aspects of my life that made those events possible. The story is such an important and intrinsic part of my own personal journeying and evolution of consciousness and should be told. It would be remiss of me not to. By choosing to share information about the Staffs I hope others can, in time, experience some of the glorious aspects of those very same Staffs for themselves.

This specific extract from my journal tells the story of my life-long star connection and how, as a result of that, the first Staff found its way to me. It goes back to the very beginning, and will give a better understanding of the amazing and revelatory universal healing content of the Staff.

firstly, the star connection

My connection with the stars is one of the most powerful and fulfilling aspects of what makes me the person I am. It sustains and nurtures me like nothing else can. I can never imagine my life without that connection. This star aspect is responsible for firing the very breath I breathe. It is a part of me which lies deeply embedded in the foundation of my soul. I am bound to my unique star connection by a familial ancestral chord.

As I think about this, I recognise the enormity and importance to me of what I have just written. This is not a recent discovery or revelation of mine. Neither is it something that has, purposefully or otherwise, remained undetected and hidden from cognitive view. I have been conscious of its existence for a very long time. As long ago as I can remember, it has been sitting quite comfortably beside me being a part of my every day living. It is something I have recognised and acknowledged at several levels throughout my entire life. The fact remains, however, that until I consciously accepted the Staff/s into my life, I did not really interact or 'do' anything specific with the star connection or it with me. Now I acknowledge the connection for the blessing it is and offer thanks daily for its inclusion in my life. I try never to be blasé, or take the connection or my understanding of it, for granted. I respect and honour this gift of connection and do not consider it as my God-given right to hold it in my possession. Just as readily as it nurtures me, so I reciprocate by nurturing it in return.

me and my great awakening

I was barely out of primary school when I first became aware of something making forays into my everyday thinking. This was something new and a little confusing. It liked inhabiting my head and infiltrating my thoughts, and generally stirring things up a little. At the time I did not really understand what that something was, or how to interpret it. I just knew that somehow something had happened which made me feel different inside. I am not even sure if I sensed this something was otherworldly or not, or if this was what everyone felt like inside as they were growing up.

It was several years later, around the time of puberty, before I recognised the feeling as a connection outwith my earthly existence. Whether puberty was a trigger or contributing factor, or whether this was purely coincidental, is debatable. I do remember around that particular time other aspects of my life beginning to make some sense to me. The powerful psychic connection with my grandmother was one of those I consciously took on board. That was something I was comfortable with. The planetary connection was different. Even then I can remember harbouring doubts, and probably a little fear, about this new dimensional input. Given the circumstances of a relatively normal upbringing, I think it was a natural reaction. The fear I was holding onto probably said more about me and my genuine lack of confidence in my own abilities to cope with the unknown than it did about any star family of mine wishing to instigate reconnection.

As I look back over that particular stage of my life again, I acknowledge that my parameters of spiritual understanding and knowing were minimal and contained. My mind was aware, but it was a confused sort of awareness. I was not awakened to a point of fully understanding higher wisdom and what that meant. Although I was still young, I did have enough understanding to realise that my life was set to change. My future depended on that. Until I recognised this simple fact, and took it on board, there would be no change. Also, I had to learn to like and embrace change. Not to do so would mean me remaining trapped in a place with little or no chance of moving forward with my life. Everything I ever knew about myself was screaming out for me to accept change. I knew I was more than ready for this necessary force in my life to swing into motion.

The years preceding the arrival of the Staffs were incredible years of discovery and acceptance of my own contributions to the universe. I had been fortunate and blessed to become a fully-fledged, paid up participant and recipient of an endless universal flow of sacred symbols, messages, information and phenomenal visions. The majority of visions registered at a personal level, but there were many more which resonated at an even deeper spiritual level. These were the ones that had the greatest impact. There was also a small percentage of visions I did not understand or connect with. It may very well have been a case of me trying too hard. I tucked away these visions for a future time when I might better understand their content.

I was given little tasters and insights into so much, without really feeling I had to commit to any one thing. The bulk of my time was taken up with exploring as many avenues as possible. Opening myself up to these wonderful new opportunities helped me to grow and become more fulfilled in my daily workings. What excited me more than anything else was the fact I knew there was so much more to come.

The arrival of the first Staff brought about even more changes. As those changes sought to secure tenure in my reality, I knew there would only ever be one outcome. The moment the connection attached itself to conscious thought, I changed. I became aware of a physical and mental shift towards a deeper more fundamental level of being. Straight away, I discovered a new inner knowing and feeling of completeness, which had been missing before. Opening up and embracing these dormant senses into everyday living was all the sustenance I needed. That part of me which had been in a state of suspended spiritual slumber was relegated once and for all to the past. I was now headed in a direction which would lead me towards a more meaningful and permanent spiritual acceptance and way of life. From that day forward, the old patterning of my life changed forever. It expanded and embraced new horizons and limitless parameters. Never once after that did my acceptance of the gift of connection waver.

Every time I think about communicating with my star/planetary aspect I am reminded of how inordinately blessed I am. I readily admit my life is greatly enriched as a direct result of recognising, embracing and opening myself up to experiencing something so uniquely special. Very rarely does the connection detract in any way from my life on an earthly plane. The exact opposite is true. It enhances my life a thousand fold. If I ever find myself spiritually challenged or threatened, or sense my faith in myself, or others, faltering I know I can seek guidance from my star connection. It is but a whisper away. Past experience has taught me that connection will enable me to bring resolution and balance to any given situation.

Trying to give substance and form to my star connection is not an easy thing to do. It cannot easily be defined. In the beginning, I sometimes got a sense and impression of the connection being like some visible detached entity hovering over and above me. I, on the other hand, resided somewhere in physical form directly beneath the actual connection. That is not the reality of it for me. That is just an imaginary something, put in place to create the illusion of separation. Although my life and its star aspect may outwardly give the impression of being removed and apart from one another, they are not. The physical goes through an instant reactivation and re-bonding process. A new, more complete image begins to emerge. There is no separation. I liken it to a planetary and earthly fusion of the highest spiritual order.

When I work with any star connection I find the 'keeping it simple' approach works best for me. By acknowledging the connection and identifying what it means to me, I am forever reminded of my ancestral planetary forefathers. Although many will disagree with me, there is not a single doubt in my mind that the stars are where I originally came from, and where I will one day return when the physical aspect of this particular lifetime on earth reaches its inevitable closure.

At times, my star connection can be all consuming, yet I would never regard this as being invasive or in any way negative. I love the fact that this precious connection has the ability to immerse itself completely with aspects of my psyche. It can hone in without advance notice, forcing me to refocus my attention, and channel my thoughts and energies directly towards the stars. Whenever that happens, nothing else exists except the stars and me. I hand myself over to the experience of connecting. We are old friends. Our energies merge and become the one we know we are.

Trying to fathom the intricacies of spiritual journeying has taken me down several pathways in the past. Once I understood about the stars and our connection it was almost as though I had somehow come home. I have always firmly believed the stars are the keepers of all known knowledge, ancient or otherwise. Creation's vast imprint and historical memory rests with, and amongst, them. They define almost every living thought or notion within the boundaries of my comprehension and understanding. I sense there is still a small sliver of opportunity, however, which could change that perception of reality. The door is not entirely closed to the exchange or sharing of a new knowledge. I believe a meeting of the minds/conscious energy can be achieved by sharing this new knowledge. The process would be like an exploratory coming together, if you like. The words 'sharing knowledge' are not difficult to understand. They mean exactly what they say. The stars may be the keepers and guardians of knowledge, but on an emotional and spiritual level I do think that communicating isn't always so definitive. There is no line drawn in the sand as far as human emotions are concerned. We can still take on board new knowledge of personal dimensions and learn from each other.

Should it choose to do so, my star connection has the ability to deflect all traces of earthly thought away from its rooted positioning. This is only ever a temporary thing, and I know not to be fearful. When my mind ceases alternating between worlds, the thoughts will find their rightful place at the forefront of my consciousness once more. Just as effortlessly as I am able to traverse and secure a firm foothold on a planetary level, so I can become grounded again and connected to all earthly pursuits. Having a foot in both worlds like this is something special and I acknowledge this.

My star connection is a constant in my life. Not a day goes by without me quite literally thanking my lucky stars for the connection. I am aware of just how much it contributes to my life here on Earth. There have been times, more so of late it has to be said, when I find myself yearning for the time when I can return to the stars and my star family. The pull and longing I have to be amongst them once more can seem overwhelming and distracting, and inordinately powerful. Instead of seeing the connection as the blessing it is, sometimes I sense it draining me on a deep emotional level. It becomes like a physical ache, gnawing away at my insides, eroding and overriding any joy I am holding in my heart. I console myself with acceptance of my soul mission and recognition that I will have to wait awhile. The timing of my return to my star family remains in my future. There is so much I have yet to accomplish. I am exactly where I need to be at this particular juncture.

As I reconcile myself to the way my life is unfolding, I know that inwardly I am not unhappy. The incredible changing times I find myself living in are unlike any other. On a spiritual level these times are quite extraordinary. As the world changes and raises its level of spiritual consciousness and awareness, I know I wouldn't want to miss one single precious minute. What a time to be alive!

the handing over of the staff

When sleep came and my nightly excursions amongst the stars got underway, something unusual happened. Through the vast expanse of cosmic motion, three figures appeared and came to stand in front of me. One of the figures was holding onto a long Staff. The appearance of the figures was so sudden and unexpected it caught me a little off balance. A spark of recognition was set into motion, but it was fleeting and nothing definitive. I knew not to be alarmed. In fact, I felt remarkably calm and in control. At some level I think I had been waiting a long time for just such a thing to happen. I had been holding onto the expectation of this event without fully understanding or necessarily knowing what the expectation was. Once the expectation materialised so too did my immediate acceptance of it.

Along with the acceptance came the inevitable bombardment of internal questioning. Who were the figures and where had they come from? Why had they suddenly made an appearance? Was there any significance to the Staff in their possession? Why did I have the distinct impression I was the sole participant in the question stakes? As I write about these figures, I find I am unable to describe or define them with a degree of accuracy that would satisfy. I have no real recollection if they were tall or short, male or female. Just when I think there might be a glimmer of insight into any physical properties, the glimmer evaporates into a barren, empty void. My memory obviously had no need for such detailed description of the figures. I do remember a couple of other things very clearly, though. All three figures stood quite still, radiating a silent mantle of magnificence. They shimmered and glowed with such a luminosity it was almost blinding. There was an unprecedented and overwhelming desire on my part to reach out and close the short distance separating us. No matter how tempting that idea might have seemed, I resisted and let it go. Whilst it evaporated into the obscurity of the ether, I remained exactly where I was and did what I do well; I waited.

Although the figures were facing me, their faces somehow remained hidden from me. I found it a little odd, but no more than that. As I stood silently trying to take it all in, it did not seem to matter too much. There was a familiarity about the figures, but it was distant and I could not quite pin it down. As I trawled the passageways of my brain, trying to tune into some small part of their essence, I could not help but sense the figures were smiling at my confusion. I wondered what sort of celestial or angelic beings they might be, and what information, if any, they might impart during their visitation. They had obviously made an appearance for a reason but what exactly was that reason? I pondered whether they were messengers from Sirius or Orion or some other distant planet. Perhaps they may even have been members of my own star family. I did not know then and even today I have no idea of their true origins or identity. What I remember most of all is that everything about their presence just seemed so right somehow. Any lingering questions I may have had on their planetary orientation therefore became redundant.

Ethereal is a word and image many people can readily identify with. They have probably at some point in their lives experienced a visual representation of what the word means to them. It is no different for me. What I find most frustrating, however, is that my memory seems capable of retaining only the ethereal element of the figures and no other. Whenever I think of them it is this singular image that springs immediately to mind. The figures themselves have clearly determined any further disclosure irrelevant. Whatever the reasoning behind that, I accept it.

The visitation of the figures lasted the entire night. At least, I am pretty sure that was how events transpired. The hours seemed to merge seamlessly into each other without a single breath being drawn. I have an understanding of communication taking place, but I cannot remember or determine if dialogue took place or not. Unusually for me, I have no memory at all of that.

Behind the veil of transparency shielding my eyes, the first light heralding the new day spread its glorious, celestial wings. Although the visitation was over and I was on my own again, I could still sense myself being bathed in the beautiful, shifting light of the three. That was not the only thing my senses were prompting me to acknowledge. Straight away, I knew something extraordinary had occurred. It wasn't just a sensation of something having taken place, I could sense immediately that something had also changed on a physical level. Before my eyes were drawn to the weight in my hands, I sensed what they were about to see. A real frisson of excitement shot through me. I indulged myself with the knowledge that whenever celestial energies made an appearance anything was possible. As my mind accommodated this realisation, it found itself adjusting to a new reality.

When I had initially seen the Staff in the hands of the figures I was conscious of the image registering inside my brain. I know that might sound odd to say it registered. There is no denying that, on the surface at least, every image or thought has to register in the consciousness, but I also believe in the existence of different levels of consciousness. Depending on one's conscious state at the time, these very same images and thoughts can end up playing games with the mind. Some will attach themselves at a much deeper level than most. The choice of whether to come and stay, or come and go again, is up to the fickleness of whatever consciousness chooses. The Staff was not playing games. It was definitely here to stay. At the time, I did not really pay too much attention to the style or physical dimensions of the Staff. I was far too busy concentrating on the figures to give it anything other than a swift, cursory glance. Now I was holding onto the very same Staff. All I could do at that point was look at the object in stunned amazement and wonder just what to make of it all.

The instant I started re-enacting every step and detail leading directly up to the Staff being in my possession my mind was flooded with defining imagery. It seemed to me as if time was standing still, and yet that was not the case. Time was evolving and 'things', for want of a better word, were happening all around me and the transient figures. I do remember sensing being on the cusp of something unfolding, yet not knowing what. When the act of planetary gift transference took place, it surprised me in its simplicity. Remarkably, even after all this time, I still have instant recall and can clearly remember the giving and the receiving of the Staff. When the figures reached out and took hold of my arms I was a ready and willing participant. What happened next seemed such a natural thing. Slowly, and with a sense of great reverence, the figures placed the Staff into my outstretched hands and proceeded to fold my fingers around it. There was no ceremony or careful words of instruction or elaborate initiation, just a simple uncomplicated handing over into my care. Then it was over.

Though no indication was given, I had an understanding that the figures had fulfilled their particular role for the evening. Now, they stood silently, just watching me. I recognised their part in the Staff's journey was complete, and our time together was drawing to a close. Without word or warning, the figures dematerialised just as swiftly as they had materialised. I felt sad, staring at the open space vacated by the three. The feeling did not last long. As if to honour just how memorable and extraordinary the night had been, my heart began to expand and radiate the pure joy it felt inside.

Now the Staff was in my possession, I felt I had a responsibility towards ensuring nothing happened to destroy the faith and trust that had been placed in me. As much as the Staff apparently now belonged to me, what did that actually mean? What was I supposed to do with it? I knew I was responsible for the safe keeping of the Staff, but again what, apart from the physical image in my head and the physical sense of form in my hands, was I protecting and from whom was I supposed to be protecting it? The questions multiplied. Of all the things which might possibly have come into my life why a Staff? Why now at this particular time? What was its purpose?

There was no instant resolution to any of those questions busily vying for attention inside my head. I intuitively knew it was far too soon to be having thoughts about the significance of the Staff as far as it related to me. For the time being, I had to try and calm the runaway thoughts and rapid fire questioning and just get used to the existence of the Staff in my reality. It was not an easy thing to do. My natural instinct was to want to know everything there was to know about this incredible gift. I do remember wondering more than once if the Staff was a part of the incredible Universal Tree of Life, connecting Mother

Earth to the celestial above. That thought lasted all of a few seconds. Perhaps the Staff was something apart from the universal connection and therefore entirely separate? Thinking about this only ended up fuelling further questions. Was the Staff meant for my sole use, or could it also be used to benefit others? How could I go about finding that out? If I were to simply reach out and physically touch people with the Staff would that trigger something or would there be a little bit more to it than that?

The thought briefly entered my head that the Staff might somehow reveal itself as an instrument of blessing and infinite wisdom. Perhaps it contained some extraordinary spiritual message for me and all of mankind? If that was the case, would it be up to me to relay its message to the rest of the world? I could not help but think that with such a magnificent object there had to be more to the Staff than a few words of blessing. What really threw me more than anything else was the not knowing. When it came right down to it, I did not have a clue about the Staff or what, if anything, it expected of me in return.

As I re-read that last sentence I realise it is not entirely accurate. I DID know. I knew, without having to be told, that the Staff would play an important role in contributing towards my future spiritual growth. Also, I already knew that in choosing to accept the gift, an expectation and understanding existed. The power of the Staff registered with me, yet I did not immediately understand the full capabilities or exact properties of it. I did, however, have a deep, inner knowing that somehow I would be the catalyst and trigger for releasing the energy and power from within the Staff. As soon as I recognised that important factor, I quickly determined that the Staff was not just for me. Hopefully it would, with time, prove to be a great blessing to others who made the decision to open their hearts and embrace its energy.

Heaven alone knows how long I sat there with the Staff, feeling its awkwardness in my hands. It seemed like an eternity. The Staff certainly was not the most comfortable thing in the world to hold onto, but that was only a small part of it. Without any obvious conscious input or guidance from me, the Staff slowly began to gently pulsate. I could sense it coming alive in my hands. Stranger still, the Staff felt as though it had a steady rhythmic constancy, just like a heartbeat. I looked on in some amount of awe as energy began to charge through the entire length of the Staff. My pulse quickened. As the energy sought to embrace me, all I could do was marvel at Spirit's generosity of so unique a gift. It was an extraordinary moment as my body experienced the energy of the Staff for the very first time.

I was stunned at the magnitude of such a gift, and more than a little intrigued when the Staff instantly began to invoke certain feelings within me. The dramatic turn of events had left me feeling a little shell-shocked. Although I had difficulty believing what my eyes were seeing, what my mind was telling me and what my body was experiencing, I realised there was more to come. A real, tangible feeling of underlying excitement fuelled my senses, urging me to discover even more about the Staff and its energy. I did not pretend to fully comprehend or understand what was taking place, but already I could tell I loved whatever that thing was doing to me.

With deliberate slowness of hand, I ran my fingers over the length and breadth of the Staff. Carved from wood, it looked remarkably like a traditional shepherd's crook. I wondered if the Staff would feel smooth, but as soon as I began to investigate I couldn't quite make up my mind. The surface gave the appearance of being slightly uneven, and there was something unusual about the crook part of the Staff. Something had been set into the wood, and although it had been skilfully done, the carving was not as seamless as I had initially thought. I turned the Staff over in order to inspect it more closely. Immediately, I could see a large, multi-faceted crystal nestling in the crook. It was spectacularly large, and as I very quickly discovered, the main powerhouse of the energy running through the Staff. I had never in my entire life seen anything so mesmerising or captivating. The crystal seemed to reach out and caress me with its beauty and an all-enveloping energy. I was completely stunned to have in my possession something so intrinsically exquisite yet powerful.

Why had the Staff been gifted to me? Out of all the people inhabiting the universe, why had I been chosen? Why was I destined to be the guardian of such a gift? I tried halting my train of thought. In the second or two it took to do that a tiny seed of doubt seized the opportunity and crept in. This wasn't really happening was it, I asked myself? As if to reconfirm and prove to myself that the Staff was not a figment of my imagination, I raised my hands and held the Staff out in front of me. It was pulsating with energy. I could feel vibrations from its very core reach out and touch me. The power of the Staff was immense. There was no real need to challenge its credibility or doubt its existence. It was there all right, and very real.

description of the staff and how its energy works

In my naivety, I believed that once I started to acquaint myself with the Staff the answers to my questions about it would immediately be forthcoming. They were not, and I was to remain in the dark, so to speak, for a little while longer. As I have stated before, over the next couple of months another three Staffs would be gifted to me by Spirit. This complicated things a great deal, and detracted my attention away from the original gift. It took several months before I could even begin to focus my undivided attention on the first Staff. I suppose, initially, the temptation was there to brandish the Staff aloft like some giant magician's wand, but the sensible and warily practical side of me stepped forward and quite literally took hold of the situation. A protracted period of discovery was about to be set into motion.

Months of coaxing followed. I questioned every thought and piece of information, no matter how small or insignificant it may originally have seemed. When that questioning did not entirely satisfy the hunger within, I questioned some more. Above all, I listened closely to what my heart was telling me. I make it sound so easy and uncomplicated, but that was not always the case. For every step I took forward, I seemed to take so very many more backwards. The Staff always determined when it was appropriate for me to be given more insight into its workings. Sometimes, weeks would pass without a single fragment or scrap of information. It was a steep learning curve as the Staff and I got to know one another. Gradually, we grew to understand the complexities and, on occasion, the simplicities of each other. A pivotal moment came when I sensed the Staff had begun to trust me and my judgement. As a result of this, I was entrusted with an intriguing piece of information. The Staff with no name now had a name. It was to be known universally as the Oberon* Staff.

Describing the Staff, and the energy contained within it, is almost a contradiction in terms. The energy is as old as Life itself, yet as far as the inhabitants of our modern day universe are concerned, it is an entirely new energy. The power and knowledge the Staff holds is immense and enduring. I have previously stated that the Staff is, to all intents and purposes, just like an ordinary shepherd's crook. There is one very obvious difference. The crook part is not made from traditional animal horn, but of wood. It is a substantial object, and measures the length between head and toe. In my case,

*see page 153 for reference.

that translates into a fraction under five foot and eight inches. The entire Staff is carved from a beautiful, pale, finely grained wood. At first glance the surface of the Staff appears to be smooth, but closer inspection clearly reveals uneven, bumpy 'bits'. When I physically feel the contours of the Staff, I begin to have doubts about just how aged the Staff actually is. My initial thoughts of when the Staff was created are, I think, inaccurate. I do not know why I have a feeling that in planetary terms the wooden element of the Staff was created specifically for the purpose of acting as a receptacle for the crystal. Separately, the Staff and the crystal traversed their own timeframes before coming together to create the whole.

The colour of the crystal set into the crook is a vibrant, deep, sparkling cobalt blue. As the tips of my fingers trace the smooth, timeless facets of the surface, I discover something quite astounding about this incredible crystal. Although it is firmly set into the underbelly of the crook, if I apply a little pressure to the crystal I can sense fractional movement. If I press more firmly, I realise the entire crystal can be removed. The very first time I slip the crystal from its resting place and hold it as a separate entity in my hands I am staggered by its celestial beauty. Rummaging around for descriptive language that would do justice to the crystal is not easy. I find myself running out of superlatives. Trying to describe or define the essence of the crystal, and the power it holds within it, becomes almost impossible. Just as difficult to articulate are my feelings as I hold the crystal, and my emotions as I try to understand it. It is difficult to avoid noticing that even with the crystal removed powerful vibrations create their own uniquely charged energy field around the Staff.

The vibrant colouring of the crystal reminds me of certain elements from other celestial workings and unions. This is the colour so often associated with the energy of Archangel Michael. Who amongst us has not at some time or other called upon Archangel Michael? When he responds with his sword of Valour and his shield of Truth he is always surrounded with the most magnificent and intense blue ray. Once you have been blessed enough to experience the energy and the colour around him, you never forget. Knowing this helps to bring a degree of comfort and reassurance. Additional information on the Staff is forthcoming. I am told that the Sirian surgeons have direct input into the energy of the Staff. There is no reason for me to doubt this in any way. I always associate that colour with their specific energy. Also, on the rare occasions I work with the somewhat mystical sounding Peacock Angel, powerful cobalt energy is present. Something else that had slipped my mind takes this opportunity and decides to prompt the cells in my memory bank. That particular colour of blue reminds me of my connection with the Hathors. The very first time I encountered the Hathors they embraced me with their amazing cobalt energy. The colour of connection with them would change over time, but the initial experience of sensing then seeing, their energy is something I will always remember.

The core energy of the Staff is quite possibly one of the purest energies around. It is to be used primarily, though not exclusively, for self-healing. I have been told that it will not throw up past lives, family issues, entities or cords needing cut. Instead, it will be recognised as a Universal Healing Energy. As it is part of Source itself, so it is part of me. This energy can be used to help the physical body and direct it towards more balanced form. It will reawaken knowledge of spiritual, celestial and metaphysical from within.

I learn with time and practice that the energy is effective in relation to distance healing, and also whilst working alongside animals. I have used it on numerous occasions on birds that had the misfortune to fly into the extensive expanse of windows overlooking my garden. Spring and summer were always the most accident-prone months. No matter where I happened to be in the house, I could nearly always hear the dreaded sound of impact. A sickening thud would be followed by silence as aerial met static. Birds would fall to the ground, stunned and immobile. Many of the birds recovered quickly and flew off, but just as many again would struggle to survive the ordeal. Normally, I would remain inside the house. I would position my wheelchair directly in front of the window and start to project the energy of the Staff onto the comatose bird. Only once did I intervene directly by going outside and lifting a limp little feathery bundle into my hands. It was one of the young chaffinch chicks which had been nesting in the shrubbery beside the old stone wall. Already in its short young life it had managed to avoid the savage clutches of the sparrow hawk which frequented my garden. It didn't seem right somehow for the chick to end up sacrificed to its own reflection and abandoned at the base of a window. If there was even the slightest chance of the bird surviving, then I would try and bring that about. When I somehow, rather miraculously, managed to scoop it up, I really thought the young fledgling was dead. Inspection revealed there was no outward sign of broken wings or damage to impossibly fragile limbs. Even better than that, there was still a beat coming from its warm body. Twenty minutes later after a constant flow of energy directed into its minute form, the bird rallied and recovered sufficiently to open its eyes and look at me. It did not panic and automatically try to break free. Instead it sat for a few minutes more, nestling quietly in the palms of my hands. With freedom firmly in its sights, the patient summoned enough energy to finally flex its wings and fly off into the distance.

To my way of thinking, if it takes five minutes or fifty minutes to try and turn things around for an injured animal or bird, or indeed any living creature, then it is time well worth taking. Every life on this planet of ours is a life worth saving. As long as the Staff continues to be in my care, and I am capable and blessed enough to be working with its amazing energy, then I will.

how to use the staff

So, how easy is it to actually activate the energy and work with the Staff? Well, therein lies the true beauty of such a gift from Spirit. Out of all my Staffs, the Oberon Staff is perhaps the least complicated to put into practical use. Bearing in mind it is a Staff of Universal Healing Energy, it is remarkably simple to use on oneself and on others should the need ever arise. With a little work, I discovered for myself just how generous the Staff can be.

I have always maintained it as good and necessary practice before starting any energy work to make the time to create sacred space. That way, the space in which I choose to work has been cleared of any negative elements that may have inadvertently decided to linger awhile. Also, by taking the time to do this one simple thing, I protect myself and honour the energies I hope to invite into my space. If you should ever find yourself drawn to work with the Oberon Staff at some point in the future, then the following guidelines will prove to be beneficial.

Take some time to create your own sacred space. Sit within that space and calm yourself in preparation for what lies ahead. Let your mind and body relax and become still. Feel your diaphragm expand as it adjusts to accommodate a steadier rhythm of breathing. Once again, make an effort to empty your head of all those wayward thoughts that almost inevitably remain attached and threaten to intrude. Be conscious only of self and the inner you, and the energy surrounding you. In your own good time, declare your intention to work only with those energies that come directly from Source. Seek the safest and best possible outcome from your connection with the Staff. Ask the Angels to protect and guide you through your experience and bring it to a safe and harmonious conclusion.

When you feel ready, try visualising the Staff in all its glory (see drawing page 130). Once you have managed to do that I want you to call the Staff to you. Keep it as simple as possible, and do not over complicate the request. If you have not worked with a Staff before, when you do make your initial request it may seem a little strange at first. That will change. With a little practice, the calling of the Staff will become effortless. As soon as you speak the words and call upon the Staff you will sense change. There will be a dramatic shift in the energy surrounding you, and you will know something wonderful is about to happen. Prepare yourself for your first glimpse of the Staff as it miraculously appears through the ether and guides itself into your hands. Those initial few seconds of realising your request has been granted will be astonishing moments.

Do not be afraid of the Staff. Sit for as long as you feel it necessary, in order to begin to feel comfortable with the Staff. Whether your eyes remain open or closed is entirely up to you and the way you choose to work with celestial energies. Really look at the way the Staff has been carved and how the crook is cushioned to support the magnificent crystal. Take in as much about this extraordinary Staff as you can. It is entirely likely that at this point you will start to sense the first gentle stirrings of the energy contained within the Staff. How does that make you feel? Are you able to connect at all with the Staff and its star/planetary energy? Do not worry too much if you do not feel the energy straight away. This is after all your experience and therefore unique to you. It will take the time it is meant to take. Both the energy and you will know exactly when to connect.

With so much going on at the same time, you may encounter difficulty in focusing the mind. That can easily happen. Even with the best intentions in the world, it is easy to become distracted from the main event. It can, at times, feel as though some speed or fast forward button is set in motion. Your mind suddenly becomes saturated with so many questions it needs instant answers to. Try not to let this interfere whilst you attempt to connect with the Staff. If you decide to act upon only one question then let it be this one. Even if you recognise and acknowledge the melee going on inside your head, do you really want that intrusion to spoil and detract from your experience of working with the energy of the Staff? Why not put those specific questions to one side for the time being and simply enjoy your experience without interruption. There will be plenty time after the event to seek more definitive answers.

During my first experience of connecting with the Staff I was acutely aware of just how highly emotional I had become. Perhaps it will be the same for you. If, as a result of your connection, you are conscious of heightened emotions coming to the surface, do not sweep those emotions to one side to be dealt with later. Instead, I would recommend facing them head on and embracing them for what they are. Now, you can move forward to the next stage of your journey with the Staff.

You may sense distant memory put out feelers to reconnect. That is alright. Just let those memories fall where they will and accept that change is on the way. This is the beginning of a great journey of discovery for you. The Staff is doing what it set out to do and is finally connecting with you.

There are no hard and fast rules when working with the Staff and its energy. Nothing is written down in stone. Because the energy is such a unique gift to the people of the world, it must be looked after. It is important to always remember to work from a place of Truth and Integrity every time the Staff is in use. We all have a responsibility to ensure the Staff is used solely for positive purposes. It must never be used for self-glorification or out of a need to massage or feed one's ego.

I feel it is essential for all the information on the Staff to be documented. As you begin to work with the Staff and discover its properties, you are effectively finding yourself playing the role of historian. Along with me, you are being invited and encouraged to write and document your own unique interpretation of the new universal history of the Staff. Even if you do not immediately consciously connect with the star aspect of the Staff, you should almost certainly be feeling incredibly blessed to be holding onto such a rare planetary gift.

It is time for you and the Staff to begin your real work together. In the first instance, feel your hands become accustomed to the weight of the Staff and the texture of the grains running through the wood. Allow your fingertips to run over the smooth, worn edges of the crystal directly beneath the crook. Take the time to trace the facets on the surface of the crystal. At this point you sense a subtle surge and expansion of the Staff's energy as it begins to slowly vibrate. Within seconds, you should physically see and feel the energy flowing more freely through the entire length of the Staff. Only then do you become fully aware of the magnitude and identity and true depth of colour of the energy. It is as if your touch alone plays the role of enabler, bringing this extraordinary crystal to life. Straight away, you find yourself experiencing a little of the power of the Staff. Your entire being is immediately immersed in, and suffused by, the energy emanating from the Staff. Only one colour in the entire colour spectrum exists and holds meaning for you. Instead of tiny baby breaths, one gigantic breath of energy wraps itself around you, bathing everything in the amazing cobalt blue rays of the crystal. It is time for the Staff to be put to use.

Other than intent, no additional words or symbols are needed. As you become accustomed to working with the Staff you may eventually decide that no hands are required at all. You can direct the Staff and its energy with intention alone. I must admit I prefer holding onto the Staff as I work with the energy. Occasionally, towards the end of a session, I might be tempted to release the Staff entirely and work directly with the crystal. Sometimes I only have to think the colour of the crystal for the work to commence.

Compared to other forms of energy work, the length of time the Staff takes to complete its task is relatively short, and normally lasts in the region of fifteen to twenty minutes. For me personally I find that the Staff works best if I can stretch out and lay down flat. I get a better sense of one uninterrupted flow of energy running through my body. If you find yourself unable to stretch out, then sit with your back in an upright position. Be sure to get yourself as comfortable as you can. Hold or place the Staff in either a horizontal or vertical position over your body. Let the Staff and your own intuition direct you. Immediately, the energy within the Staff will intensify. The shift is significant. All your nerve endings and senses are activated as you begin to feel the core power of the Staff for the very first time. At this point you can do one of two things. You can decide to use the Staff with the crystal intact, or you can remove the crystal from the crook of the Staff and hold it in your hand. Whichever way you end up using the Staff, the outcome remains the same.

One of the main functions and purposes of the Staff is to bring a sense of balance to the body. In the process of doing this the Staff journeys and visits all the chakra points, joining them up and clearing them of any obstructions or negative elements. Imbalances that may have occurred in the physical and mental over the years are sought out. Anything that creates imbalance and confusion, and no longer serves a positive purpose, is addressed. The Staff isolates those specific aspects that have manifested as problems, and the energy from the crystal helps restore and repair them. With no interruption or separation, the flow of energy steadily works its way up and through those damaged or out of sync areas of the body until it becomes one balanced and continuous line of pure energy.

At the end of this extract I will briefly describe the effects the Staff has on each individual chakra point, but for the time being I will continue with the extract.

Once you feel the Staff come to life, point it directly at your feet and let the energy begin to work on you. Stay connected to each chakra point for as long as you feel the need, before moving on to the next. You intuitively know when the timing is right. As the Staff moves upwards, you can, if you think it necessary, set a further intention to hold onto the energy from the previous chakra point. Every time the Staff or the crystal is moved from one position to another, the sensations it elicits continues on already treated parts of the body. The higher up the chakra scale you go, the more extraordinary the feelings of balance and spiritual connection. Savour these moments. Linger a little and let the whole experience become a part of you. I remember the time I had a sense of complete union with the energy. It was such a momentous experience and sensation I felt sure the energy had reached deep inside me and left its imprint on my soul. If you are lucky enough to experience something similar, then open your heart even wider and embrace that. Do not be in too much of a hurry to rush forward to the next chakra point. Learn to control the impulse and stay in that space a while longer. As the Staff reaches its final destination at your crown chakra, you literally feel every individual link in the chakra chain join up and vibrate with the full force of the Staff's extraordinary energy. Once you experience that you know the decision you made to take your time was the right one.

No closing down or sweeping is needed at the end of the Staff's work. After such a beautiful healing, a big thank you for receiving so special a gift is always good. When you come to the end of the treatment you should be feeling happy and balanced, and aligned with your star connection. Some of you may also be having an additional unique experience. Once all the chakras have been treated by the Staff, and your body has absorbed and retained the energy of the crystal, you may find something amazing happening. I have to caution myself that perhaps you will not. Because of my own experiences whilst using the Staff, I firmly believe it is entirely possible that you may experience something similar to me. I see no reason at all why you should not discover for yourself what it feels like to become one with the Staff and the energy. It does not happen on every occasion the Staff is in use, but when it does you definitely cannot forget the experience in a hurry.

My very first experience of becoming one with the energy is something I treasure. Without going way over the spiritual top, it certainly proved a life-enhancing moment of some import and significance. I can recall exactly how it made me feel at the time. As I sensed myself gradually begin to merge with the energy, my entire body just melted away into nothingness until all that remained was the energy. It was extraordinary.

Only by experiencing such a thing for yourself are you able to get any real sense of what my words mean. Even then, there is no guarantee your experience will even faintly resemble my experience. If you do have a similar experience to mine, however, only then can you begin to have a much more significant understanding and knowing of the true magnitude of the Oberon Staff and its powerful planetary energy. That is what makes the Staff such a very special gift to the universe. Whatever the Staff determines your experience to be, SO IT WILL BE.

Always listen to the energy of the Staff and what it is telling you. Never try and force any form of energy work. It simply is not going to work and you are left extremely disappointed as a result. You can nearly always discover for yourself how to achieve the best possible results, both for yourself and others you may wish to help. I am sure the more you invite the Staff into your life, then the greater the rewards. There may come a time when you sense you want to try and expand the boundaries of the energy. So long as you feel comfortable and confident working with the Staff, then there is nothing to stop you. Experiment with the parameters of the energy. You may have experience of working with sound. Try incorporating the energy along with sound wave elements and see what happens. The Staff is an incredible implement for self-use, but it is also ok to have some fun with the energy.

The final part of the Staff's participation in the whole process/ session has arrived. What happens to the Staff now your daily work together is done? Before you return the Staff to the safety of Spirit and the ether, you must ensure that the Staff is as you first found it. If you remove the crystal from the crook of the Staff in order to work with the energy that way, then you must make sure that the crystal is restored to its original positioning in the crook. Only then can you finally release the Staff back to its home in the etheric.

Having connected with the Staff and invited it into your life, know in your heart that the Staff is a part of you forever. It can return through the ether to you at any time. You only have to make the request for reconnection. Think the colour of the energy and visualise the Staff. By accepting there is no separation, that is enough for the Staff to return to you once again.

how the staff affects the individual chakra points

Feet and knees: When you become uncertain of your next move, this helps you take the next step. Absorb the energy, feel it, get a true sense of its copious abilities. If you are feeling stuck in your tracks and need assistance, the Staff will help guide you on your way. The time has now come to step out into the world and follow the path you have chosen for yourself. Go forward with courage.

Base: Breathe in the colour and feel it touch all your reproductive organs. Be aware that actual movement within this specific area of your body can occur. It is similar in many ways to an expectant mother feeling the baby inside her womb reach out and reposition itself for the first time. This is a re-awakening at a very basic level. New aspects of self are beginning to unfold. Dormant energies are reactivated and begin to re emerge. Enjoy the warming, almost liquid-like, sensation of the energy as it spreads through you. Archangel Michael and the Sirian surgeons are particularly strong here.

Solar: The absolute powerhouse of your energy, and the centre of your physical body. Recharge run down batteries here and feel them surge with the pure energy of the Staff. Sometimes, you may sense a 'top up' here is all that is needed. It is always better to take time to treat all the chakra points. Again, on occasions, be aware of the possibility of input from the Sirian surgeons.

Heart: Feel the energy spread across your entire chest area. Imagine your heart as an exquisite, pale pink camellia slowly opening up and revealing its beauty for the first time. Prepare to accept the energy of the Staff as it places itself at the centremost point of the flower. Let the delicate petals gradually close in around the energy. Absorb its essence. Take the energy into your heart and let it become part of you and your daily life. Embrace everything it has to offer you.

Throat: Open up the strictures of your vocal chords and let your Truth be told. Let your voice be heard by all. Speak out and spread the word. Only by communicating and opening up to new spiritual avenues of dialogue will the truths of life be heard. This is of paramount importance.

Third eye: This will help to open your eyes further. You will start to visualise more, and become even more aware of energies evolving and how those energies affect your life. Really explore and expand your horizons. The rewards will be enormous and will also help remove any blinkered views you may be holding onto. Be prepared to see 'fully' what is in front of you. Numerous realisations are confirmed.

Crown: Help to reawaken those parts of your brain that remain inert and in a state of limbo. Physically, you may sense your head 'doing something a little strange'. You might even get the sensation of adjustment as its capacity momentarily expands to receive more planetary and spiritual information. It can be an odd sensation. The energy comes directly from Source. At times, you may feel unable to absorb all of the energy. Relax and soak it up.

An aside: At the end of a treatment, if you have not already done so, then place the crystal between both hands. It will help release your creative powers. This may be writing or other forms of artistic input. Remember the importance of keeping a record of your experience, and also of passing on as much relevant information as you can, so that others can benefit from learning about the Staff and its energy.

*The name of the Staff (see page 143). When I was given a name for the Staff I was a little confused. It struck me as being odd. Why would a Staff be named after a character in a play written by William Shakespeare? Why was there no obvious planetary association to the name? A decade further down the track I had all but forgotten my initial reservations about the name of the Staff. Imagine my consternation when surfing the internet I came across quite by chance (no such thing as chance I hear you say) an interesting and hitherto unknown (to me) fact. On January 11th 1787 William Herschel made an incredible discovery. Looking through his telescope he came upon something both he and his fellow astronomers could only ever dream of finding. That thing was a new moon. This new find turned out to be an outermost major moon of the planet Uranus. Later that same day, Herschel made his second great discovery. There was a second moon. Initially, these moons were referred to as Uranus II and Uranus IV.

In 1852, the son of the late William Herschel named both moons. He named the first moon Oberon and the second one Titania. When I read about Herschel and discovered the name that was eventually chosen for the new moon everything seemed to just click together somehow. I am not saying there is a connection between the Staff or the moon, but I do find it interesting.

The way I work with the energy of the Staff has not altered in any way since learning there is a moon out there with the same name as the Staff. I continue to use the Staff as I have always done; with gratitude.

Extract no. 8:
Crystal pyramid, Faeries in a dell, The magic of Unicorn and Earth healing labyrinths

I have almost finished a lengthy section of additional material into my memory journal when I am distracted and guided towards my crystals. Unlike the majority of people I know who are drawn to crystal energy, I do not have in my possession a large array of crystals. My collection remains relatively small and numbers around fifty or so. It is pretty rare for me to have all my crystals openly displayed or on show all the time. Occasionally, when I feel the need arise, I will rest certain crystals for short periods of time. Some may simply be wrapped up and put away, whilst others are briefly returned to nature and buried in the soil outside. The majority of my crystals are instantly recognisable. Others are a little more unusual. All my crystals have at some time or other played a role in the energy work I carry out.

I have often heard it said that crystals seek out their own

guardians and I wouldn't necessarily disagree with that. Each and every one of my crystals has specific resonance and meaning for me. Marvelling once more at their unique qualities, I am reminded of so many memorable experiences I have had using these crystals. As my eyes feast on the smooth glistening edges of crystal temptation, three crystals immediately stand out from the others. In a bid to be chosen, each begins to vie for my attention. Normally, my intuition directs me towards one particular crystal. This time it does not. Which of the three should I choose? Because I cannot make up my mind I decide to look at all three of them; a single large and irregular shaped chunk of rose quartz crystal, a sphere of dark glistening labradorite and a beautiful, almost flawless, crystal quartz sphere. Reaching forward, my fingertips relax and I touch each of them briefly. One by one I pick them up and allow their individual icy coolness to rest against the palms of my hands. Immediately I sense familiar gentle stirrings of recognition and a deep inner knowing returns. I love that sensation and the way my feelings are so easily invoked. It comes as no surprise. We are old friends, the crystals and me.

As swiftly as that reconnection awakens within so my work begins. Within minutes of tuning into the crystals I am aware of subtle changes and shifts in my energy field. As the weighty rose quartz settles into the softened crevices of my hands, images slowly start to emerge and seep into my consciousness. I sit quietly letting the sensation wash over me. Within seconds of the imagery flooding my senses hundreds, if not thousands, of large elongated rose quartz crystals, each the size of an average adult human, begin to fall like giant sculptures from the heavens above. The momentum they gain as they descend is nothing short of astonishing. Spinning and rotating at extraordinary speed through this liquid vertical force field, the crystals flash a blinding kaleidoscopic brilliance. I am rooted to the spot, completely transfixed. Each individual crystal appears to reach out and tease with a solid silent promise of intent. The sheer magnitude of such a force raining down around me makes my body ache with the effort involved in remaining upright. The sound of this thunderous descent bombards my senses from every angle, and makes the earth shudder alarmingly beneath my feet. As the vibrations take on a life of their own and start to ricochet outwards, I feel their power surge through the soles of my feet then upward through my entire body. This deafening descent continues for some period of time before finally coming to a shuddering, heart stopping halt. An all-enveloping silence ensues.

I can see and sense the foundations of a magnificent crystal structure spreading out and taking root. Somehow, I have an intuitive understanding that all the individual crystals have a collective consciousness, in tune and in total harmony with each other. It is at this moment the crystals, which are strewn so haphazardly on the ground, choose to come together and take on the form of a pyramid of extraordinary proportions and dimension. What a truly magnificent sight it is. I am conscious of light and powerful forces emanating from the structure. All are quite phenomenal. Some have a familiarity about them, while others are unlike anything I have previously encountered. All I can do is stand in wonder as the structure invites and draws me towards it. I know it is time to commit and play my part.

What I say now may not resonate or sit comfortably with others who have not experienced such things for themselves. I know that as soon as I step into the centre of this glistening edifice I am freely giving permission for the crystals to release and impart their ancient wisdom and knowledge to me. This holds no real fear. Just as I have done on numerous occasions in the past, I become a willing participant and step into this munificent gift from Spirit. By embracing and opening myself up to receiving such a gift, I feel my life force instantly expand. Although I cannot accurately define or interpret the full degree of the ancient planetary and star wisdom bestowed on me, I know the words and their meaning have left their imprint. It may not be visible, but it is there nonetheless. I become aware of higher wisdom and am immersed in a deeper more meaningful level of spiritual connection and consciousness. Downloading of information from Spirit is not something I ever take for granted. I know without a shadow of a doubt just how truly blessed I am.

the enchanted dell

After my crystal experience, I sit quietly in the residual energy. I am content to do this. Time passes. Gradually, I sense my surroundings change and I find myself being transported to a realm of lush scenic landscape. Immediately, I am reminded of my Celtic ancestry. Everything about this destination makes my heart want to smile. Whatever energy is responsible for inviting me into this wondrous place I can get a very real feel of it. It is a tangible living something, which is opening its arms wide to embrace me. I sense all I have to do is reach out and instantly I will become a part of the light, fun and laughter beneath this pleasure-fuelled place. It is a wonderfully liberating sensation.

My body goes limp as it relaxes into the space. I can feel my eyes soften around the edges as I try to take in my new, verdant surroundings. In the distance, blue misty mountains loom large and magnificent. Dominating the skyline, they merge seamlessly into the soft rolling fields of nature. There is nothing to hear but the silence wrapping itself around me. It is picture-card perfection.

I am just beginning to get my bearings when suddenly, a few feet off to the left, a large hillock springs up through the ground. It is covered in a thick luscious carpet of moss. When the figure of a man suddenly appears and sits firmly astride the hillock I am caught slightly off guard. Riveted to the spot, all I can do is stare at him. Who is he? Even more curiously, what is he? My initial gut instinct finds me veering towards thoughts of leprechauns and faerie folk. Although I have knowledge of both through my workings with nature and nature spirits, I have never experienced either leprechauns or faerie persons before in any physical form. If my prediction is accurate then this will be a first for me. I am really excited at such a possibility.

Focusing on what is unfolding is not as easy as it first appears. I have an overriding sense of having stumbled upon a fantastical scene from a classic Walt Disney movie. Any second I half expect Bambi and other woodland creatures to make an appearance. That does not happen. Remaining seated, the figure stares right back at me. Beneath overgrown, silvered, clumpy brows, green eyes sparkle and flash at me. Heightened, rosy-glossed cheeks expand as his mouth relaxes into an irrepressible dimpled grin. There can be no mistaking the slightly bemused look on my face. I can tell my companion finds my confusion hilarious. As his hands come forward to rest on the copious girth of his fairly nondescript earth-coloured suit, I notice for the first time the large glistening buttons adorning his chequered waistcoat. They look to me like an assortment of amethyst and pale green coloured rock crystals. Every breath he takes is carefully orchestrated to show the crystals off in the best possible way. From somewhere deep inside, the figure's expansive belly begins to shake and rumble and take on a life of its own. Within seconds he is roaring with uncontrollable laughter. He is so busy rocking back and forth and kicking his spectacularly polished, sturdy, round-toed boots in the air he almost falls off the hillock. Enough balance is retained for some silent message of inclusion to pass between us. I cannot help myself. It is now my turn to laugh out loud and join in the sheer exuberance and joy of the moment.

An air of some special enchanted thing about to unravel filters through and around us. I can almost feel the magic at work. When he of no name says my name I am intrigued. As if commanded by some royal decree, he motions me to come forward and sit by his side. I am more than happy to comply. It is as I take my first step towards him that he decides to share his name with me. He is known as Eridron and he is King of the Faeries. Whilst I am absorbing and digesting this piece of information he stands up and in a few strides shortens the distance between us. I am surprised to see he is only marginally shorter than me. We walk slowly through the landscaped idyll until we reach a beautiful low-branched, silver-leafed tree. Sitting underneath the tree's canopy weaving long pale grasses, hawthorn berries and rosehips together is a beautiful faerie figure. Eridron tells me she is Galitia, Queen of the Faeries. Everything about her demeanour and dress is exquisite. From the finest gossamer threads of her flowing gown to the silver tasselled slippers on her tiny feet, she is quite captivating. As I see and feel her energy reach out towards me I am completely transfixed by the sensation and the emotions rising up within me. Eridron and I move forward and join her under the tree. She stands up to embrace us. For my part it is a profound moment. Acknowledging and recognising the true beauty and meaning of energies uniting is something quite special. It doesn't stop there. The collective connection joining all three of us is powerful and filled to the brim with promises of things yet to be.

Straight away, I can tell there has been a shift in my perception. Suddenly, the sights and sounds and smells of this magical faerie dell come alive around me. Every living thing projects a life-enhancing, spine-tingling energy. It is an extraordinary thing to experience faerie realm and earthly realm coming together. I feel incredibly blessed to be a part of something so unique.

Surrounded by such beauty and the bond of kinsmanship, we sit quietly in the space and time. I remember us speaking of many things, none of which has retained permanence in my memory bank. Something I do specifically remember speaking of in great detail is Mother Nature and her extraordinary powers and gifts to mankind. We are constantly reminded of her magnanimous giving nature and generosity of spirit. Whether it is the mountainous, snow-capped peaks encircling the world, or the deepest ravines of the oceans floors and all the spaces in between, the great Earth Mother chooses to honour us daily with her blessings. Without any attachment of burden or sense of obligation the very least we can do is to honour her in return. The faerie realm has always responded to such generous gifts by doing all it can to work with the energies nature provides. Recently reawakened souls inhabiting earth at this juncture should do no less. If we ever hope to truly evolve spiritually and step consciously into evolution, then we must realise we all have an intrinsic part to play in making that our reality.

Hours drift and melt away. We continue to sit under the tree until the sun starts to settle on the fading contours of the blue misty mountains. Like the softest brush from a mother's lips, a gentle breeze whispers through the leaves of the silvered, overhanging branches. I am aware of a subtle shift in the energy surrounding us and can sense change skirting around the edges of this magical faerie dell experience. There is no time to react to the slight feeling of anxiety rising up inside me. One minute the three of us are looking into each other's eyes then suddenly, without warning, the King and Queen of the faeries are gone and I am on my own once again.

To say I am shocked by our parting would be wrong. There is no real reason for me to be saddened by the inevitability of the departure. I think my initial reaction is to imagine I have lost some rare and precious thing. The reality is the complete opposite. I haven't lost anything at all. The whole experience has left me feeling really happy and full of life. To have been granted such access into the faerie realm is a privilege and something I will never forget. Though my time with the faeries might have seemed short, the gratitude I feel inside me is immense. Memories of time and space and words shared will live on in me as I continue the incredible journey of my life mission.

Before I finish writing this extract on my faerie experience, words of faerie wisdom spoken by Eridron drift back into my consciousness. He tells me that I am to, "Play by the Light of the Night, Dance on Toes in the Frosted Grass". I love those words and the imagery they invoke. They remind me to always acknowledge the inner child and celebrate life and the sense of playfulness and joy within oneself.

magical, mystical unicorn

Through ancient mystical lands and ethereal mists of time, the hazy outline of a creature slowly starts to emerge. At first I find it hard to determine what it is. My heartbeat quickens as promise of something magical about to unfold reaches out to touch my senses. The narrow woodland landscape shifts and begins to expand. Slowly, but with great purpose, the mists shrouding the scene lift and part. Stretching out in front of me I can see feint indentations sitting proudly on a springy moss pathway. The scene is bathed in brilliant translucent light. Fearful of being distracted, my eyes continue to focus on the creature standing in the distance. Somehow it must hear or sense my presence. Slowly it turns sideways and acknowledges me. A defining image emerges. Hardly believing what I am seeing, my breath momentarily falters and catches in my throat. Smaller than a traditional shire horse, yet larger and sturdier than a mountain pony, there can be no mistaking the identity of the creature. Against a backdrop of magnificent woodland, the majestic messenger slowly turns its glorious distinctive profile towards me. I am, for once, at a loss for words. The scene in front of me is like something taken straight off the pages of an otherworldly fantasy. For me, however, this is no dreamtime or fictional story book experience. This is me living and experiencing my reality. When I am invited to work with celestial energies it always thrills me. Any affiliation I have with star energy leaves me with a sense of having come home. Perhaps because I never imagine such a rare and privileged reality will ever present itself I am thrown a little. What am I supposed to do now? With no clear guidance, I continue to gaze in wide-eyed wonder at the creature. Almost immediately an underlying feeling rises up to test my resolve. Is this magical experience about to slip away through my fingers? Controlling and holding onto the experience becomes my sole focus. Hoping to absorb every single nuance and aspect of this precious gift, I step fully into the space and the moment. I am not disappointed.

The light emanating from the creature is as spectacular as anything I have previously seen. When I feel myself being drawn towards and into that light I offer no resistance. I am in complete awe of what is taking place. Looking at my surroundings, I see thousands of minuscule starbursts explode at the same time. They create a staggering floating star shower. Whilst the energy flashes and glistens and shimmers I can feel it embrace and nourish me. I have to keep reminding myself what extraordinary spiritual times I am living in. Anything is possible. This experience IS real. I know the creature can sense my confusion. As if on cue, it responds by telepathically communicating with me. An invitation for me to walk forward is made.

Still slightly incredulous, I find myself standing beside a

magnificent unicorn. Although I have memory of unicorn energy, it is distant. This is the first and only time in my current lifetime that a unicorn has fully revealed itself to me. It is a monumentally profound experience. In a heartbeat I feel a surge of emotions start to build up inside me. I recognise these emotions are complex and hold out little or no hope of unravelling their mysteries at this particular time.

Although what I say next may sound clichéd to some, in my heart I know it is not. Intense, silvered-blue eyes waste no time in searching out mine. Reaching deep into my soul, these compelling orbs of gentle otherworldly knowledge and persuasion encourage me to reveal my Truth. I don't have to think twice about placing my innermost self into the safe keeping of this spiritual messenger. Everything about me is laid bare before the unicorn. It sees me and everything I am. Time stands still. A feeling of something akin to euphoria sweeps through me. I can sense myself being supported and cocooned in a beautiful diaphanous blanket of star energy. Its purity and power is breathtaking. Still holding my gaze, the unicorn invites me to reconnect, not just by thought but also by touch. I cannot turn away from such an invitation.

My initial apprehension about reaching out and touching the unicorn quickly evaporates, and I feel myself relax into the reality. Whilst I am hesitant of going anywhere near the glorious, glistening regal head and invitational horn of the unicorn, I have no hesitation in reaching forward to touch the side of its glowing luminous flank. I don't know why I am surprised to feel warmth beneath the flesh. What is it I am expecting? The unicorn's silver stranded mane is thicker and ropier than I imagined it would be and there is so much of it. It is luxurious, and soft as finest eastern silk to touch. As I continue to run my fingers through this magnificent overly-long mane, something happens. I can feel a gentle tingling sensation charge through my whole body. It is not uncomfortable. Initially, it feels like a mild electric shock. As I stand, quietly experiencing the exchange of energies with the unicorn, it is soon forgotten.

Immersed in the sensations of this incredible experience, I still have an awareness of the unicorn continuing to communicate with me. Amidst all this wonder, I am invited to do what I wanted to do in the very beginning. I am given permission to reach out and touch the horn of the unicorn. What an extraordinary moment. There is no need for a second invitation.

The unicorn could not have given a greater or more precious gift. Holding its gaze, I reach out and curl my fingers around the base of the magnificent horn. I don't quite know what I am expecting, but when I touch the horn, nothing is as I imagine. Straight away, I can feel powerful vibrations. Energy is pounding through the entire length of the horn. The heart of the universe beats gently within this cornucopian mystery. Ancient knowledge and wisdom, and so many other things besides, flood my senses and trigger memories. Visions and symbols of past lives in Lemuria and Atlantis reach out to embrace me. Giant, crystalline, aqua-coloured crystals, resting for millennia on the floors of the oceans, vie for my attention. They are desperate to impart their knowledge. My heart races at the memory. When glimpses of things in the future make themselves known, I am accepting. A constant stream of information passes into and through me. Whilst it is tempting to assume that I can accommodate the knowledge of the world without limitation, I know I don't believe that. Somewhere in the back of my mind is the understanding that the unicorn will protect me from information overload. It will not give me more than I can actually cope with or hope to process.

Standing for an indeterminable time in this otherworldly domain/ state of being, absorbing the energy and bathing in the rays of the star-fuelled light, I immerse myself totally in the unique hypnotic energy of this wondrous creature. My heart feels as though it might explode at any moment. Every single part of me is blessed and filled to capacity with Light and Love and Grace. What a gift I have received this day.

I can feel closure beckoning. My special time with the unicorn is ending. By sharing and imparting the knowledge I will need on my journey, the unicorn has fulfilled its precious mission. Without so much as a backwards glance, the unicorn turns and walks away. The ethereal mists close in around the scene, and just as magically and wonderfully as the unicorn arrives, it departs to the celestial realms once more.

labyrinth earth healing

For several days leading up to 10/10/10 I give considerable thought as to how best to honour this special day. Initially, I think it a little unusual when not one, but three, extremely large joined-up infinity symbols come to mind. I am guided to think about projecting all three symbols onto the narrow but lengthy stretch of grass in my back garden. On the day I will step into and walk all three symbols. When I query the purpose of three connected symbols I am told the first is to represent self, the second earth, the third the stars. Within seconds of receiving this information the symbols disperse. They are replaced by images of three large separate labyrinths also representing self, earth, and the stars. A short while later sees me considering a third option. I am to walk around two separate labyrinths. One will represent and be used to walk the path for earth healing, and the second for planetary healing. It is a little confusing, but no more than that. I know whatever happens on the day will be the most appropriate; no matter.

As it turns out, when the day arrives I end up creating one enormous labyrinth. I step into the first of its seven circles. Within a matter of only a few yards I am forced to come to a halt. The path is blocked by two disturbing images slowly rising up from the ground in front of me. Much as I might wish otherwise, I cannot ignore the images and know I must face up to them.

Famine in war torn Rwanda, and harrowing scenes of the utmost misery and deprivation in parts of Ethiopia, stare right back at me. My heart sinks. Yet again, I see survival or not being played out on the big screen of life. Two countries held hostage at the mercy of nature. The pressure of surviving to live another day is increased as nature's grip over the people intensifies. Nothing is ever made easy in the sub-Saharan countries. To the world at large, the people of these regions are most commonly portrayed as victims of circumstances not entirely of their own making. To a degree that may be true. One of the most distressing aspects of all of this is the inability to see a solution or way forward. I have to ask myself If the world at large cannot see the possibility of things improving, what in the name of hell can I do to make a difference? Determined to at least try to be a positive influence, and inject energy into the situation, I calm the disturbing thoughts and set to work. Calling on my Earth Healing Staff (gifted to me by Spirit many years ago) I take a few minutes to reflect and reconnect with its powerful energy and the astonishing domed crystal concealed at its top. Light needs to replace the darkness currently permeating the very foundations of these two nations. Before I can make any progress, first of all I must address that particular challenge. I ask for continued support for the health and relief agencies in assisting as many people as possible, in as many areas as possible. As I continue to work with the energy of the Staff, the more daunting the realisation of my participation becomes.

To the majority, starving populations are a constant reminder of the disparity amongst nations, and the incomprehensible divide between those who have and those who have not. Instead of coming to grips with starvation and deprivation, the whole issue rolls relentlessly forward like some out of control mammoth. One might expect that input to rectify the situation would result in a decrease in the numbers of people starving, yet every year the figures continue to escalate. Outwardly, there seems little realistic chance of reining it in and bringing it under control. No matter how much we wish otherwise, the reality is that starvation and everything associated with it continues to gain momentum.

Moments of relief from daily starvation are scarce. Just as quickly as those moments materialise, so they dematerialise, and the daily fight for survival rears its head once more. People from many nations dedicate their lives to bringing an end to hunger and malnutrition. If even one life is saved as a result of their commitment then that person has been saved to play a future role in the divine plan of life. Those who choose to merely stand back and observe can make a huge difference by standing alongside the hungry and dispossessed, and by committing to honour and support those who choose to fight to live.

As I project the image and state the intention to alleviate hunger, I know that it will take more than intent to eradicate this problem; so much more is needed. It is not only the people of these two nations in need of resuscitation and rescue. The earth upon which they tread also needs to have its thirst quenched and spirit nurtured back to life. That means rejuvenation and regeneration of epic proportions. Can it be done? Climatically and financially, it appears an almost impossible undertaking, even with outside assistance, yet I cannot help but feel that while people hold onto hope they hold onto the possibility that things CAN and WILL change. When your belly is empty and distended, and the ground beneath your feet scorched and blistered by the rays of the sun, hope is all you have left. None of us can have any real understanding of what that feels like. We have never experienced such deprivation.

I feel ashamed and more than a little embarrassed by my privileged existence, when I ask that the people of Rwanda and Ethiopia be granted even greater courage and strength than they currently possess, in order to sustain them until such time as they can take tiny steps towards a future without hunger. My thoughts turn inwards and I chastise myself. Who am I kidding? What do I know about courage like that? The whole world has to recognise that millions of people struggle daily to survive. Some extraordinary thing within those very people forces them to take another breath towards living, no matter how difficult or impossible their lives might be. Change has to happen. We all have to believe in that, otherwise what is the point? If there is to be any chance at all of the world progressing as one, then a commitment from successful wealthy nations will be required to set the wheels in motion.

With one final Blessing I continue walking until I complete my first circle.

The second circle of the labyrinth deals with deforestation in the Amazon basin and in Indonesia. Where to start, exactly? How does one go about addressing, let alone reversing, a situation of such wanton and commercial destruction? Guidance comes along with haunting images. Huge scarred swathes of open land stretch out for hundreds of miles in all directions. The destruction is hideous. Both legal and illegal loggers have decimated the landscape. Whilst the majority of the world sits back and pretends nothing untoward is happening, tens, if not hundreds, of thousands of trees and their life-giving emissions are at the mercy of industrial chainsaws on a daily basis. Huge areas of productive land lie abandoned, denuded of their 'for profit' bounty. Where beauty once graced the landscape, destruction now stares back. My stomach turns over.

I ask for the protection of all living things, including animals still living on the land and in the rivers. Birds inhabiting the forest canopies that still remain are not forgotten. When it comes to the smallest creatures and insects of the forest floor, I visualise them rebuilding areas currently affected, and those areas most likely to be affected in the immediate future. I seek to try and redress the imbalance deforestation has created by putting in place the intention for a resurgence of all organic life, and a definitive pattern of new growth in the areas already destroyed. Finally, I ask the universe to bring together all companies involved in the logging industry to help guide them towards finding more renewable and sustainable sources, where supply does not bring about such wide-scale destruction. I also encourage a global review of current practices and see what can be gifted to humanity, rather than stolen from humanity.

I walk forward into the third circle not knowing quite what will happen next.

Bees are what happen, or to be more specific, the decimation and death throes of bees in numerous countries around the world. I know that here in Scotland a few years ago there were major problems with bee colonies and mite infestation; whether it was a case of foreign bees somehow migrating to these shores in search of a food supply, or new strains of bees being accidently imported, the infestations threatened to completely wipe out existing colonies.

Few people realise that something like seventy to eighty per cent of plants depend on bees for pollination. If those plants come under sustained and aggressive attack from pesticides and parasites it won't take long for the bees to disappear off the face of the Earth. Small, isolated pockets might manage to escape and hold on, but sadly they too will come under threat as the world realises just what it has lost.

Not so very long ago, I saw a distressing documentary on television about bees. Tens of thousands of hives in the United States were under attack from some unidentified source. Whatever the origin of the source, it proved to be completely ruthless and indiscriminate. It swept through colonies across the length and breadth of the States. Just as swiftly as the hives were rotated and moved to pastures new, it became apparent that the silent but deadly destroyer of the bees had followed. Apart from the beekeepers of the world, few people were aware of this sinister turn of events, or the implications for the future of the bees. It was a catastrophe of gargantuan proportions, and one that should have left the world reeling.

Seldom can I recollect seeing so many grown men break down and cry as they surveyed millions upon millions of their bees lying dead on the ground. Other beekeepers were equally distraught when they returned to find hundreds of their hives completely empty. There were no signs of bees anywhere, or any indication of where the bees might be. They seemed to have quite literally done a vanishing act and disappeared into thin air. It was heart breaking.

Although it might have seemed that way at the time, all was not lost. That great provider, The Universe, responded. Help from the other side of the world was at hand. The Australian government put in place a rescue mission. Because of rigid regulatory controls within Australia about importation of animal or plant life, the hives in Australia were completely free from infection or mite infestation. Australian bees were exported to the States to kick-start the revival of the bee population.

I ask for this programme to be successful and disease free, and for the bees of the world to multiply and continue to make glorious honey for our breakfast tables. I remain standing with my eyes closed for a few minutes more visualising and projecting this happening.

As I step into the fourth circle I am confronted with images of pollution and its impact on our planet. Whilst there are many countries around the world with serious ecological and environmental issues, I am, on this occasion, guided to focus on one nation in particular...China. Images quickly fill my mind. Rightly or wrongly, these are the images so often portrayed of late to western eyes via television and the media. Under the auspices of progress, I can see an unprecedented level of change taking place. Legions of industrial bulldozers plough and blast their way through the length and breadth of the country on a monumental scale. The situation is what it is. China is no different to any other country. Economies have to compete and move with the times. I am not passing judgement, however I do get a sense that the rapid progress of industrialisation in China comes at a price regardless of the human or ecological cost. Images of enormous factories loom up before me. Chimneys taller than skyscraper buildings belch out noxious fumes twenty-four hours a day, obliterating the sun's rays and polluting the atmosphere in the process. This form of expansion is unstoppable. It is resolute in its determination to move forward, and it stands aside for no one. Land that was once farmed is steamrollered and industrialised. Often, the negative aspects of all this outweighs the positive. Lungs, which once breathed in clear country air, now suffer from breathing in fumes they have no recognition or understanding of. The old way of life and living is gradually and systematically being eroded. A new age has dawned. It is time to move forward. Even though some might regard my actions presumptuous, for the next few minutes or so I feel all I can do is to concentrate on sending light and love to China and its people.

Entering the fifth circle, the energy around me seems to soften a little and become more fluid. It feels light and bursting with life. I don't have to wait long before a message filters through. The oceans and the waters of the world need to be cleansed and purified. I find myself smiling as I remember a discussion I had with a friend of mine several days earlier. We spoke about getting a small group of people together at two separate locations to do some energy work in relation to water. Straight away, I know what I must do and where I must focus my energy. Collecting my thoughts, I visualise a beach someway down the coast from where I now live. It used to be a favourite place to walk the dog and go paddling in rock pools with the children when they were younger. At high tide, the water crashes in over the rocks surrounding the little bay. When the tide turns, the powerful forces of nature suck the water right back out, first of all into the Forth then eventually the North Sea. I stand for quite a while with my Earth Staff, calling energies to unite in cleansing this one small stretch of beautiful coastline. As I visualise this happening, I can feel the intensity and power of the energies at work. It is always a humbling experience.

With my work at the coastline over, I make my way inland to my second location. This is a very special place for a lot of people. Hidden away from view is an ancient, mystical place so beloved by pagans and druids over the centuries. Nowadays, people seek out its mysteries and amazing connection with the energies of nature. The area is heavily wooded and steep in parts, and slopes down into a natural dell formation. In the springtime, the dell is carpeted in acres of bluebells. Several months later, autumn weaves its own magic spell. Running through the centre of the dell is a river. Narrowing and expanding in places, its course inevitably runs cross-country and down to the sea. The dell has a strong pull on my senses, so perhaps that is why I love working with the energies of the river so much. Surrounded by spirits of nature, I bless the river and encourage it to flow clear and clean over the lands it inhabits. Before I say my farewells, I thank the river and the ocean for the beauty and the daily bounty they provide me.

When I step into the sixth circle I have no forewarning of what is to happen. The message I receive seems simple enough, yet is anything but simple. I am encouraged to pay close attention to the mountains encircling the world. Somewhere in time, a fracturing and disconnection of energies has occurred. These majestic spines of the world need to be coaxed into activation and reconnection. Why is it all made to sound so easy? In response to my own questioning, the instruction I am given is instant, and perhaps by necessity, startlingly uncomplicated. Immediately, I see a child's 'join up the dots' colouring in book right in front of me. I turn to a page that is easily identifiable as a large map of the world. Holding a soft wax crayon between my fingers, I systematically begin to join up all the dots. I have knowledge of most of the mountain ranges. This helps a great deal when it comes to colouring them in. With regards to the location of the others I make a calculated, and hopefully accurate, guess.

It takes a little while to imagine the powerful energies of the mountain ranges. From deep within the bowels of the earth supporting the mountains, to the tips of the peaks hiding in the clouds above, the energies reach out, searching for that moment of reconnection. I spend a lot of time setting the intention and concentrating on making that incredible intention a reality.

The seventh circle sees me returning to places where I have done a great deal of energy work over the last couple of decades. They are the San Andreas Fault line and the Earth's grid. Both of these are in need of constant monitoring, and require major inputs of restorative energy far exceeding anything we as inhabitants of earth can bring. It does not stop me from trying to do what I can. The fissures and fractures of the tectonic boundary between the Pacific plate and the North American plate are well known. Running through the length and breadth of California, almost dissecting it in half in the process, the Fault stretches for hundreds of miles in either direction. Because of the complexity and challenge facing me, I know I am going to need some help with this. I decide to call on the Blessing Staff to assist me. Though imagining the true extent of the Fault's destructive elements is not easy, picturing the land and the rugged contours of the Fault line is relatively straightforward. Staff in hand, the energy begins to flow. I begin to direct Light and Blessings directly onto this gargantuan scar of nature. The unimaginable destructive forces deep beneath the surface of the line absorb the Light and its life-giving energy. I continue working with the Staff until it lets me know when it is time to stop.

After a few brief moments of reflection, I encourage the incredible beauty of the Earth's grid to fill my senses. This complex never-ending mass of depth and perpetual movement is in a constant state of exploration and evolution. Whilst Light takes my breath away, colours defying description take on a life of their own. Geometric shapes and structures fill every conceivable space. Their size is staggering. I am astounded and mesmerised by the scale of everything. Energies float and bend and vibrate. Waves of sound bounce effortlessly off the structures. The sight ignites a spark of something almost primordial deep within me. Observing all the components coming together to create this invisible living security blanket around our world makes me feel insignificant and emotional. What a phenomenal sight the grid is. Every time I am privileged enough to experience its energy, my reaction is the same. It never fails to amaze and excite my senses. There is more. Something I often sensed, but could never fully understand or accept before, is given meaning and the recognition it deserves.

With the light of the grid surrounding and supporting me, I waste no time in calling the Jupiter Planetary Staff to me. This is the last Staff gifted to me by Spirit. Its energy is normally incredibly complicated to work with. On this occasion, however, everything is made so much easier for me. The combination of planetary colours and energies come through straight away. Work begins immediately. With no guidance as to which specific section or structure to focus on, I send wave after wave of Light and powerful energy directly into the entire structure of the Grid's mainframe. I am so busy concentrating on channelling the energy that I lose all sense of time. Gradually, the energy in the Staff begins to close down. I give my thanks to the Staff and return to the earthly plane once more. My work and journey on the labyrinth is complete. The day, which promised so much, has delivered the magic of the universe directly into the centre of all that is me. What a joy. What a blessing.

Extract no. 9:
Experiencing the energies of angels and other celestial beings

No matter how often I ask myself the 'angel' question the response remains unflinching in its stubbornness to reveal anything tangible. At what point in my life did angels first register and put down roots in my consciousness? Try as I might, I cannot come up with any definitive answer. As I search for a way through the maze of celestial information stored in the burgeoning receptacle classified as memory, I decide to give in and revisit the question.

It would be natural enough to suppose that some sort of visual recognition of a celestial image might be responsible for setting the wheels in revelatory motion. Then again, perhaps it was a lot simpler than a residual visual imprint and I just had a knowing that angels existed. Cautioning against accepting the first 'maybe' thought from the memory bank, I determine to take my time and sift through any information that springs to mind.

the first gentle stirrings

I had not quite reached double figures when I first recognised subtle changes to the way I thought and felt about certain things I was doing. Whether these events were speeded up somehow as a result of a strong attachment to my psychic grandmother I don't suppose I will ever really know. All I knew at the time was that inside my head my thought process was a bit of a jumble and all over the place. As I tried to absorb what was happening, things started to shift and new patterns began to emerge and take form. I feel certain now that this was the start of my intuitive senses coming to the fore.

By choosing to acknowledge that, I wonder if that very same intuitive awakening was somehow responsible for steering me in the direction of angelic energies, or had childlike curiosity guided me towards those energies at a much earlier stage of my life? I think about this for a while. Secreted away somewhere in the recesses of my brain, something familiar stirs from its protracted slumber. Although the memory is faint, it shows a determination to be recognised. My mind clears and makes way for instant primary recall. Visions of wondrous, fantastical dreamscapes resurface. Accompanying those visions is a palpable sense of mysticism and expectant mystery. Remembrances come flooding back. As I let them wash over me, I live the experiences all over again. Were these extraordinary visions and accompanying sense of nurture my first real insights into realms inhabited by celestial beings?

Time gives the sense of standing still as I am transported back to those moments in my dreams where all physical restraints are banished. I marvel once more at just how effortlessly I fly and soar. The sense of freedom and exhilaration that this elicits fills me with a sense of absolute wonder. Moving again through those timeless, ethereal mists of uncharted realms with such apparent ease forces me to rethink the whole scenario. Have I been rather naive holding onto the belief I was flying solo, or has some unknown source been assisting me. Through all these experiences have angels been supporting me and flying by my side? Time has absorbed most of my recollections, yet one aspect of these dreamscapes has continued to live with me to this day. Although I cannot recall encountering any celestial beings per se, I remember sensing and knowing I was never truly alone on my dreamtime journeying. Perhaps acknowledging this one fact is recognition enough for me of angelic existence? I quickly determine that in all probability it is not enough.

Trying to coax the memory of a time when the wheels of cognitive thought on angels took hold is not easy. The memory is reluctant to accommodate, and I struggle to find an answer. When that first cohesive thought on angels materialised did it occur at a very specific moment in my life or did some significant thing trigger the event? If I go along with the premise of angelic existence, what if anything, was it that alerted me to that existence in the first place? Were my senses somehow awakened to the possibility of angels, or did something just happen out of the blue to make me aware of their presence? Though I have no recollection of any physical manifestation of angels, was I somehow able to sense and actually feel their energy for myself on a physical level? Without the certainty of knowing that angels inhabited my reality, how was it even possible for me to answer any of these questions with any degree of accuracy?

On reflection, the whole process of angels introducing themselves into my life was probably a gradual thing. I suspect the idea of them may have been supplanted in my brain by others who had more than a passing awareness and understanding of them. Of course, there is also the possibility that someone chose to share their own personal experiences of angelic encounters. If that did indeed happen, I wonder if that person was guided or instructed to tell me, or did their intuition sense the timing was right and I simply needed to know? There are so many questions. It frustrates me a little that I cannot reach any real conclusion. I ask myself one final time if I came to recognise the possibility of some celestial energy, or did I already possess an inherent silent awareness and acceptance long before the thought found its way to the forefront of my consciousness?

I suppose with hindsight, and knowing what I now know, angelic energies have been around me all my life. From the very moment the precious seed of new life secured itself within the womb of my mother, to the moment I came into this world, I was under the protection of invisible angelic forces. Discovering that birth was just the beginning of a life under the guardianship and protection of a whole host of angels was a wake up call of prodigious proportions.

As I am writing this down a thought stops me in my tracks. I realise, quite possibly for the first time, that I do not know if my parents ever believed in angels. They certainly believed in miracles and in a God, but when it came to angels I am not so sure. It strikes me as unusual that in a lifetime of knowing them so well I cannot recall us ever having discussed angels. Did they exist within the parameters of my parents' lives or not? I suppose when they were both still alive it was not something I ever gave much thought to. There was no real need or inclination to do so. It is only now they are no longer here I accept I will never know the answer.

When I was growing up, introductions to anything otherworldly tended to enter my consciousness through the pages of storybooks. References to angels were, as far as I can recall, few and far between. The first physical recollection I can accurately say I have of seeing angels occurred when I was around eight or nine years old. These winged, celestial beings were not flying freely and looking down on me from the heavens above. Instead, I extricated them from an old chipped tobacco tin belonging to my father. They were so lightweight I could hold them in the palm of my hands.

The moulded paper cut outs had clean, crisp edges. They were highly prized and came in several sizes and colours. Along with many of my school friends, I was galvanised into collecting them for my scrapbooks. The larger the scrap, the more sought after it became. When I had too many of one particular type of scrap I would exchange for something not already in my possession. I can remember the cherubs definitely being much more popular scraps than the images of the angels. Perhaps it was all to do with the colours that were used. In my mind's eye I can still see chubby, dimpled little arms supporting cherubic rotundity. Cascading golden locks framed glowing pink cheeks and all-encompassing smiles. Resting gently on the shoulders of each image were wonderful concoctions of pearly white wings. As they sat atop floating clouds of Canaletto skies, these heavenly representations of perfection vied with each other in their bid to be chosen. The angels, on the other hand, tended to be either stark interpretations harking back to the early days of medieval art, or faded, pallid copies from renaissance frescos. Generally speaking, the angels seemed dowdy when compared to the cherubs. There was always an air of suppressed solemnity about most of the angel images. I suppose to a child this might somehow have made them less attractive. Somewhere along the line they must have struck a chord and held some appeal for me because I can remember collecting them. For a short period of time in my life I became an avid collector. Accessorising the blank pages of scrapbooks with heavenly images became a passion.

Around the same time as I was acquiring my glossy images I started attending Sunday school. I can remember I was always kitted out in my finest 'Sunday best'. As my father was away for a large part of my childhood, it was left to my mother to escort me to the snug little vestry at the back of the church. En route we would walk through the ancient walled churchyard. Chiselled out features of magnificent figures with folded, feathered wings would look back at me from the sanctity of the weathered headstones. Although they were quite different to the images I was used to seeing and collecting, there was a silent understanding that they came under the generic term known as angels. Occasionally, my mind would also register small stone replicas of angelic beings with wings guarding the graves of the very young. Seeing these carvings did not however necessarily equate to my understanding angels any better, or what it was they represented.

At some level these artistic depictions did somehow lodge inside my diminutive young brain, but because they had no direct impact or bearing on me or my life, the reality was the images held very little meaning for me. In those very early days my attention span was not yet fully developed. As a result, it had its limitations. Without even thinking about it, I suppose I was doing what so many would attribute today as living in and for the moment. That particular state of mind never lasted long. Once my curiosity was satisfied it would seek out the quickest and most direct route to pastures new. Within seconds of being in the moment, unless I encountered something utterly riveting, I would lose interest. Like a lot of children my age I had not yet learnt the art of patience or appreciation. As a result, I couldn't wait to discover what exciting thing lay in wait for me around the next bend. No matter how temporary a diversion that might prove to be, the temptation was generally enough. My fickle, untrained mind would rapidly adjust and prepare to embrace the next experience.

Each year, as Christmas beckoned, images of angels seemed to multiply. They were everywhere. In recognising that I suppose I must have moved on from my years of not consciously engaging with angels to a place of quiet acceptance. Generally, these visions of winged innocence and pristine purity would appear in glossy nativity scenes on a whole array of Christmas cards and other yuletide ephemera. The thicker the cards, the glossier the image portrayed. Some angels had outstretched wings, others seemed to glisten and shine with the light from their golden halos. Whilst the brilliance of their image seemed to invite inclusion, their beatific smiles reached out in silent, encompassing embrace.

Most children saw this time of year as a celebration, and not so much the giving, but certainly the receiving of gifts. All of us knew the special story behind the celebration. It was easy to get caught up in the wonder of a special child being born in a manger far away in a distant land. The celebrations weren't just for the children. Parents could join in too. I can remember having a real sense of something magical happening when all the adults would stand up in church and sing about this new born child. Their voices were happy. The way I look at it now, it does not matter terribly much whether in the process of rejoicing they gave recognition to angelic presence or not. The fact they were happy and were able to share and express those joyful emotions made everyone feel happy.

There is another memory of Christmas and angels that lingers. Since others have in all probability had similar experiences and memories I decide to make a short detour and record it. When I was growing up, my school always held a Christmas service. All the children would practice for weeks trying to fine tune our young voices and make everything as perfect as we could. The main part of the carol service was always the re-enactment of the birth of Jesus. It would be played out in all its spectacular, faltering glory for all to see. I can still feel the heightened sense of anticipation surrounding the event. Every one of us longed to dress up and participate. We were desperate to have a starring role in the production. Who would the teacher choose to be a Joseph or a Mary or one of the wise men? When it came to the parts of the angels we all knew who was likely to get those parts. It was always the prettiest girls in the class who were chosen. As would-be angel eyes sparkled in expectant wonder, tumbling locks would await their very own halo of glistening silver tinsel. Opaque, gossamer-framed wings were attached with slippery threads of shiny new ribbon. The image of celestial magnificence was complete.

I am not sure why I find myself wanting to write about this next little episode. In the end I decide that since it involves aspects of heavenly things, and since it has sprung to mind, I need no other justification or reason for its inclusion in the extracts.

I could only have been around eight years old when I went to my first ever funeral. It was during the long summer holidays staying at my aunt and uncle's in the north of Scotland. They were not really blood relations, but I called them aunt and uncle anyway. I can clearly remember my young cousins accompanying me to the sombre occasion. Although my tender years seemed to preclude an awareness of direct angelic involvement in my life, I think I did somehow sense some other 'thing' was evolving. Perhaps intuition was testing me with its first tentative foray into my consciousness. I really do not know. Although I cannot confirm it, I am almost sure all three of us could feel things changing. It is difficult to put into words. Somehow, we had a knowing that some unknown element was subtly shifting our energy around and making its presence known to us. It felt like some invisible hand was reaching out to guide us. We felt comfortable being guided. Nothing was expected from us in return.

Young as we were, we had already heard about funerals. We even knew what we were supposed to do at a funeral. Being in possession of one vital piece of information did of course help considerably in bolstering our confidence. All of us were unwavering in our belief that the word with the special meaning would help us. Although it sounded a sad word on the few rare occasions we had actually heard anyone use it, somehow that word really seemed to help. The word that was so special to everyone was 'Heaven'.

My cousins and I had heard people say that Heaven was a place somewhere in the sky where you could send anything which had died. What exactly happened when the dead thing got there none of us could have said. We quite simply did not know. Before anything could find its way to Heaven we knew a special ceremony would have to take place. Each of us would have to help dig a hole in the ground then say something serious or sing a song from a book people took to church on Sundays. Our little trio felt confident in our ability to do that. We could help send the dead thing to Heaven. After that, it would be up to the dead thing to find its own way through the gate we had heard about.

The body of the fledgling lay at an odd angle where the stones met the grassy verge. As I picked it up to show the others, I could tell straight away it was dead. Its eyes were covered by a flimsy, transparent sheen of death and its body was cold and stiff. I recoiled as my finger accidently touched the blood on the side of its short, oyster-coloured beak. Though a minuscule congealed globule had formed, it still felt sticky to the touch. As we took turns to stroke and smooth the soft downy feathers on its breast, we all felt sad that this little bird would never again know the freedom of flying in the skies above.

With the greatest care and solemnity we placed the lifeless form into the hastily dug hole near the back door. My aunt came out and watched us. What grave little faces we had as we covered the bird with the freshly tilled soil. We collected an assortment of the sweetest smelling petals from fallen flower heads and scattered them over the flattened surface of the newly filled in hole. There was just one final thing left to do. As our tuneless little voices chanted indecipherable words and sounds of ceremony, we placed two discarded ice-lolly sticks across the carpet of petals. In the absence of angels, we did our best to help the fledgling go to Heaven.

adult connections

It was only when I set out on my spiritual journeying and opened my heart and mind more fully that I began experiencing angelic energies coming into my life with any degree of regularity. Whether my God connection was reignited as a result of this was, for whatever reason, something I found myself reluctant to pursue. Religion and I have had an interesting, and at times challenging, history of connecting then disconnecting. It was during one of these latter disconnected phases that I cautiously invited angels to connect with me. I wasn't disappointed. They accepted the invitation. At a time when I sensed others couldn't or wouldn't hear my words, the angels were the only ones who did.

I could feel my limited parameters shift and my perspective on life and perception of life swiftly expand to embrace the new. These events triggered a domino effect, which saw my life accelerating into a tumultuous type of freefall, and my horizons stretch far beyond anything I had ever imagined possible. Daily living suddenly became a great deal more thought provoking and interesting. Some might assume from this that I aligned myself and discovered religion again as a result of angels appearing. They would be wrong in that assumption. When angels became a positive aspect in my life I didn't automatically feel the need to accept God or any specific religion as part of the package. Instead, I gladly attuned myself to what angels brought into my life and moved forward with grace and gratitude in my heart. God and I would make further discoveries about each other and reconnect again at a later date and destination.

Recognising and accepting the existence of angels was a pivotal moment on my spiritual pathway. Abandoning some of the misguided misconceptions I had been holding onto was one of the best things I could ever have done. I learnt to let go of fear of the unknown and embrace what I had been gifted by the angels. Part of their gift to me was a renewed sense of peace and deeper spiritual understanding. They also opened my eyes and gave me the vision to walk towards a new and irrefutable love surrounding and supporting my heart. This placed no restrictions on whom and where and at what time it should love. As I gave my heart up to being open, and accepting of anything and everything crossing its path, all the barriers and limitations I had previously erected around my heart came crashing down.

Choosing to live from a place of Truth and Faith changed me and the way I saw myself. It freed me up and liberated everything that went into helping me remove the mask of illusion. There was no place for ego in this new living. All past pretence of self was removed and I discovered the reality of the new emergent person who would inhabit me on both a physical and spiritual level.

I can remember feeling slightly apprehensive yet excited when I asked for the name of my guardian angel for the very first time. I don't think I even got as far as finishing the question in my head. Without any hesitation in proceedings two things happened. A name was given, then within seconds of this revelation, my vision was immersed in the most glorious, luscious colour imaginable. It wrapped itself around me and filled me with a sense of incredible tenderness and nurture. My first reaction was one of surprise. Not only could I see this incredible colour, I could also sense the colour of the energy. It seemed to suffuse all conscious thought and go to the centre of all that was me. Something else happened which ended up surprising me just as much. I realised straight away that my angel was no ordinary angel. I had been presented with the name of a mighty archangel.

I don't know if I was disappointed or not that no clear image attached itself to the voice which had just spoken. Although I could sense the presence of a large, fluid energy it simply wasn't possible to get a physical impression in my head of my archangel. I wondered if what I was sensing was normal or not. Maybe my mind was playing tricks on me? My first encounter with angelic form wasn't quite as clear cut as I thought it might be. Having nothing to compare it with only succeeded in further confusion. Perhaps angels weren't in the business of showing their faces, I surmised. Maybe that was just the way it was going to be with me and any angels I encountered. Maybe the wings and feather bit would come later.

I was still a little unsettled from my encounter. Doubt reared up and faced me head on. 'Did that really just happen?' I asked myself. Had it really been as easy as asking for an angel to appear and hey presto one actually did? Just to make sure I wasn't mistaken, I asked the question for a second time. The colour around me intensified, filling every conceivable optical space in my line of vision. I found myself having to partially close my eyes against the blinding shafts of brilliance. The voice and the name of the angel remained the same. I remember at the time feeling almost foolish and embarrassed that I had ever doubted the existence of a guardian angel. Surely what I had just experienced was proof enough?

From that moment on I felt as though I had been given the green light. After that initial introduction angels very quickly became a conscious part of my life. They took up residency, not just in my mind but also in my heart. Wherever I turned there was a silent acknowledgement and awareness of their angelic presence and energy. It didn't seem to matter whether it was day or night. All I had to do was think about them and their energy would reach out and touch me. From the first teasing sensation of a cheek being gently brushed, to the barely there hint and smell of lavender, I could always sense their presence. If I ever had moments of doubting myself and my interaction with angelic energies the angels would always reassure me. Just before they appeared to me an image of vibrant forget-me-nots would fill my mind.

I constantly hear people say that angels love to be invited into the lives of people who genuinely seek to make contact. With a little practice I soon got the hang of inviting them into my life. I am so glad that I did. Not only have they enriched my life they have also helped to expand my sense of consciousness and spiritual existence and open me up to some truly wonderful experiences.

lasting impressions

As I seek to revisit my connection and collective experiences with angels, something unusual and quite puzzling happens. I find it difficult to marshal my thoughts and write anything cohesive. This extract really should be the easiest one to put down on paper, yet the angels are really making me delve deeper and think about my words and what it is I really want to say. Is there anything that has not already been said or written about much more eloquently than I ever could? Conscious of the copious amounts of written word on angels already out there in the public domain, my mind is suddenly swamped with thoughts and seemingly insightful quotes from other people's experiences. Titles of best selling books filter through into my consciousness, but this fails to bring the clarity I seek and only succeeds in muddying the waters even further.

My mind falters and begins to extricate itself from thoughts of personal angelic experiences. Finally, it attaches itself to something far less fleeting. I find my senses tune into the recent groundswell in the number of journeying souls who have awakened over the last decade or so. Much of this is down in part to angels and spirituality in general being talked about much more readily. Thanks to the internet and a few enlightened publishing houses, access to material on angelic and celestial encounters is far more accessible. The fear people once had of being ridiculed and marginalised for believing in angels has been greatly reduced. Without realising exactly when it happened, a growing number of people have been led back to living from a place of Truth in their hearts. They have rediscovered Faith in whatever God they once believed. Faith has become the absolute bedrock of their personal existence. People are no longer fearful of expressing themselves and admitting they believe in celestial energies.

I like to think the spiritual emergence and reawakening so many have experienced is more in keeping with an evolutionary and planetary rebirth. In recognition of this my heart wants to celebrate. I am so at peace with myself and where I am with my life that I feel like doing giant cartwheels in the sky, and dancing amongst the stars and encouraging the whole world to look on and join me. To think that the random selfless actions of others are responsible for bringing about the much needed raising of the world's consciousness is, to me at least, nothing short of miraculous. This unprecedented chain of events is already helping regenerate this incredible planet of ours, and in the process restore mankind to its rightful place. How astonishing is that?

I begin slowly thinking about the ever-increasing number of people from all walks of life who have come forward to tell the world about their personal connection with angels. I admire them enormously. By coming forward and speaking their Truth, and showing their Faith in angels they have made a commitment that can only be applauded. Thinking of those who have chosen to openly stand by their beliefs like that reminds me once more how brave these souls are. Taking the steps of discovery for themselves takes courage. Acknowledging they have reached that place of divine acceptance is a reward that is almost beyond parallel.

A growing number of people out there today have chosen to dedicate their entire lives to the study of angels. These scholars are generally happy to speak openly and share their knowledge with others. There is so much to learn about angels and other celestial energies.

Because they are possibly more embedded in our consciousness, it comes as no surprise to me that the majority of people tend to focus more on the archangels and angels. If you were to ask anyone who works with angelic energy they will elaborate and probably tell you about the existence of hierarchical ranking and celestial order. This can and does vary a little. On the few rare occasions anyone asks me to elaborate a little on this hierarchy I always consciously choose the one that resonates with me the most. Depending on which order is deemed most suitable, the order is more or less as follows. At the top of the list, and sitting closest to God, are the Seraphims and Cherubims. These are closely followed by the Dominions, Thrones, Powers, Principalities, Virtues, Archangels, and finally, Angels. No matter which way anyone looks at it that is quite some list! So, where and how should one start?

When it comes right down to the nuts and bolts of spiritual journeying, each of us has choices and decisions to make. As we seek to find our way through to a path of our liking we can blindly adopt the teachings of others as the God-given Truth. It is, of course, important to remember and recognise alternative viewpoints to these teachings do exist. This presents us with the opportunity of exploring any or all celestial avenues opening up before us. It doesn't have to be an either or situation. Because we as individuals are blessed with free will and free choice in our lives we can make the decision to embrace absolutely everything on offer, or nothing at all.

Stories and anecdotal information on angels is easy to find these days. Most bookshops have a section of authors to choose from. Whilst others experiences of angelic connection is interesting, I decide it is probably better if I stick with what I know and what I have actually experienced.

My initial experience of celestial energy was with an archangel, so I should probably start by describing the magnificence of archangels. No sooner has the thought surfaced than I find myself inwardly smiling. It is an odd, almost irreverent, moment as my thoughts turn to angelic hierarchy. At the very beginning of all creation, when God was putting the heavenly structures in place, did he always intend to automatically place archangels closer to Himself than those apparently relegated to the lower rungs of the angelic ladder? Was it an essential part of the grand plan to even have a hierarchy? Perhaps this was something which evolved in the minds of ancient scholars so that some sense could be made of the knowledge they had accumulated in their lifetimes? Who amongst us really knows for certain the workings of the master of all creation? An image of archangels quickly begins to form in my head and puts a halt to my musings. I am calm and comforted by the thought that perhaps these very same archangels are right at this very moment looking down on me and smiling along with me.

For several seconds my mind refuses to settle down and starts to dart and dance inside my head. Distracted, I find it impossible to respond to the question about which angelic energies to write about. Hoping to put something constructive about angels onto paper is going to require focus and concentration from me. I try again.

So, I ask myself, would it be better for me to elaborate more on what I choose to call the angels of the days, or should I focus solely on those angels I feel I have a special connection with? Maybe I should be writing specifically about the serenity and grace projected by the healing angels and the earth angels who work tirelessly to protect the universe we inhabit. I suppose if I did that I might possibly end up reducing the amount of time I spend writing about the family angels. These angels play a vital role in communicating with each other to help resolve matters between family members. They are masters at reconciliation and restoring balance.

It would certainly be remiss of me if I failed to mention the impact of my encounters with angels and crystals. Over a long period of time angels have presented me with several spectacular crystal gifts. Memories of those cherished moments are never far away. When at the very outset of my spiritual journeying angels asked me if I would become the keeper of a magnificent oval aqua crystal, which once belonged to the dolphins of Atlantis, I readily accepted. The same was true when I was gifted my first two Staffs. They contained extraordinarily powerful crystals. The impact these crystals had on the energy work I carried out daily was dramatic and lasting.

Angels and crystals always seem to me to be a divine dynamic combination. Recently, I acquired an ancient, gloriously carved rose quartz crystal key from an angelic source. Sparkling and flashing with rainbow prisms and angelic images, the key was as intriguing as it was beautiful. My hand reached out in silent acceptance of this unusually large and weighty offering. Immediately, I was given clear and precise instruction on what to do with the gift. It was no small thing. I had the opportunity of making another life-altering decision. Would I accept the challenge? More importantly, did I want to? I knew as soon as the key was handed over into my care that I had committed myself to accepting the conditions which came along with that. If I decided to go ahead and use the key it would, I was told, assist in unlocking my future. Should I follow the instructions I had been given or not? Did I have the courage to insert the key into two spheres from my own crystal collection?

Whilst I was not conscious of any real overriding desire to be shown my future, my curiosity was aroused. The angels had presented me with the key for a reason, and although I recognised that, I didn't necessarily think that reason and the outcome would be determined by angelic guidance. When I thought about this I suppose a case could have been made about the angels testing me in some way. That may very well have been true, but I wasn't convinced. To me, the gift was simply that...a gift. It would be up to me what I chose to do with the gift. At that point I do recall pausing to deliberate what I should do next. I knew what my heart was saying, but my head was lagging a little behind. One thing helped to nudge me forward. When the angels handed me the gift they hadn't said anything at all about me being able to see or know what that future was. All I did know with any degree of certainty was the gift would unlock my future. That was it. The decision was mine to make. Was I tempted? Of course I was! Few, I feel, would have chosen to ignore such a celestial offering.

Sitting alongside, yet apart from, the other crystals in my small crystal collection were two spheres. The smaller of the two had a starry, brooding intensity about it and was made of labradorite. The other, much larger, sphere was clear quartz and, depending which way I held it on any given day, full of delicate, iridescent angel wings. Because of the properties contained in this sphere it had always been a particular favourite of mine.

Although the key did seem impossibly large for the task ahead, I knew everything would work as the angelic energies intended. Accessing the centre of each sphere was an astonishing experience. When the oversized key locked into, then turned inside the spheres, several things happened in quick succession. Multi-faceted coloured lights and shooting starbursts of energy seemed to explode around me, filling my senses. There was no arguing the fact that the revelations on my future made a startling visual display. As to what revelations actually registered with me on a wholly conscious level I simply could not have said. My future may have been unlocked, but I had no real awareness or knowing of that future. That was fine with me.

When I found myself being sucked into the epicentre of a spinning, spiralling vortex of extraordinary energy and motion, I put up no resistance. In the space of my reality it took only seconds for every fragment of the energy around me to fade and fall away. Light and Time merged. The key unlocking my future was absorbed by the larger of the spheres. I was so immersed in oneness nothing else existed for me.

It is only as I continue filtering through other angelic memories that I suddenly remember the stopping-me-in-my-tracks energy with rainbow coloured stripes. At first sighting the mass of energy gave the impression of having no beginning or ending. Though beautiful to look at, I found the intensity of the colours and their jumbled movement a little distracting. As a result it was difficult to really focus. Within seconds, thousands of rainbow stripes began to come together and take on shape. A faint outline of a pair of massive, irregular wings gradually emerged. There was nothing else apart from these two magnificent wings. I had never encountered energy like that before. At first I wondered how energy could take on such form. I never ever did discover the true identity of Raziel and his angelic energy until many years later. The saying about coming to things when we are meant to was never truer than in this instance.

It would, to me anyway, seem almost an injustice if I forgot the incredible work of the angels who assist with helping lost souls move on to the Light. How often over the years have I connected with them and worked alongside them? Also, I know the angels who look over the safe arrival and delivery of some of the most enlightened children the world has ever known have to have a mention here in these writings. What an extraordinary blessing these children are. They have such an important role to play in all our futures.

Over the last decade or so I have had a strong affiliation with angels who magically and mysteriously assist my soft, and at times rather breathless, voice to effortlessly harmonise with celestial sound. Never before or since have I sounded quite so glorious or in tune! Should I elaborate more on that aspect of angelic connection? The choices are limitless. Therein lies my dilemma. A blanket of reluctance slowly descends to shadow my memories. Nothing specific comes rushing forward to be recognised or written about.

and so the journey begins

Angelic energies have been more than generous in assisting and offering guidance to me on my spiritual path. From the curious, more formal dialect and ancient sounding phraseology in which 'Thee' and 'Thou' and 'Dearest Beloved' are commonplace, to the insightful instruction spoken in current tongue, angels have stood firmly by my side from day one. They have been, and continue to be, unwavering in their support. In saying this I am conscious not to give the impression that my connection with angels is something I ever take for granted. By sharing my experiences and writing about them I hope I am not coming across as seeming to be more deserving of angelic presence in my life than anyone else. There is nothing so very special about me that would warrant being singled out by the angels. Angels embrace EVERYONE seeking to make a connection with them. It does not matter what path you may have already trodden, if you call out to the angels they will come to you. If you open your heart to them they will know.

In the beginning I was always under the assumption that each person had one guardian angel who stayed with them throughout their entire life. As if that wasn't blessing enough, everyone also had their own personal spirit guides. Each fulfilled specific purposes in life. When, from the very outset, it became clear to me that I had more than one guardian angel watching over me, I knew I was extremely blessed. It didn't stop there, however. All too soon I discovered there were angels for practically every possible situation and occasion. They were practically lining up just waiting for an invitation. I wasn't alone in my belief or understanding of this. Those who have similarly connected with angels will know exactly what I am talking about.

Every time I make a connection with angels they almost always come bearing gifts. In each visitation something precious will be revealed. The gift might be a few words of encouragement or, occasionally, one single word. Sometimes, it is purely the strength the presence of angels manages to evoke. There has never been a time when angelic energy has failed me. When I request assistance it is always immediately given. It may not be in the way I anticipate it happening, but it does always happen.

One of the first angel events to leave a lasting impression on me was a weekend workshop held in my home. There was a larger than normal group attending. After a chatter-laden, high-decibel-level lunch we began the afternoon of the second day by reconvening and sitting in a large circle. The majority of us were in a quiet, reflective mood. Closing our eyes and embracing the stillness, we enjoyed the experience of simply being. No words were necessary. As well as being all enveloping, the silence reached out in blessing. Inhaling the marvel of oneness and fulfilment enabled us to sense and experience what it was to live in the moment.

When the shift in energy came it was subtle but still discernible. I am sure we have all experienced those rare moments when advanced sensory insight and nervous, mind-tingling expectation suddenly takes over and teases the senses. I pretty much knew straight away that we as a group were on the cusp of something exceptional. The whole atmosphere in the room had magnified and taken on an entirely different dimension. By then, many of the group were aware of the shift. This is my experience of what happened next.

I could physically sense the circle in which we were sitting begin to expand. Immediately to my left, a gap of several feet appeared. Within a matter of a few seconds, it was all change again. Without any indication of what was coming next, every inch of the room was suddenly bathed in Light of such clarity and intensity it almost defied description. I have experienced celestial Light many times before, but nothing prepared me for this particular Light on this particular day. Its warmth and depth and brilliance washed over me and went straight into my heart in waves of exquisite blessing and nurture. Only the most magnificent celestial energies could be responsible for gifting this Light. I knew I was in the presence of something unique that day.

First, there was the awareness. Recognition of the senses swiftly followed. Ever so slowly, one ascended master after another began to brush past my shoulder and walk towards the centre of the circle. I had an intuitive understanding and knowing who some of them were, but the majority remained a complete mystery to me. All I could do was look on in sheer astonishment at this turn of events. Hundreds of ascended masters walked past me into the rapidly expanding mass at the centre of the room. Somehow there was still space left over for many more to file silently past me. It was an extraordinary sight. The whole thing being played out before me should have been an impossibility, but I knew in my heart it wasn't. This acceptance did not entirely dissuade the ever-practical side of me from humorously wondering how it was possible for the room to expand to make way for all these spectacular spiritual Beings of Light. The answer never did come.

The procession of ascended masters gradually tailed off and was replaced by a steady stream of angels and archangels gliding gently towards the centre of the room. Apart from these celestial energies and the incredible Light they brought with them, nothing else existed within the realm of my own consciousness. Everyone at the workshop had silently faded away. The only presence I was aware of was the ascended masters, the angels and me.

I don't know how long I sat there in that space with The Light supporting me and filling my senses. The whole concept of time turned on its head and became redundant. Not so much as a trace remained. Like one of those effortless, trailing whispers of a cloud, it evaporated into a vast and never-ending void.

As soon as thought saw the opening and entered my consciousness, I knew I had allowed being in the moment to slip through my fingers. It was lost to me. Light took on a different mantle and changed into a softer glowing, golden Light. I watched all the ascended masters and angels smile and turn their faces inwards towards an angel who had walked right into the centre of their circle. Everything went into slow motion after that. Whilst ascended masters and angels looked on, the angel at the centre started to walk towards me. The feeling of sheer joy and celestial euphoria surrounding me almost threatened to overwhelm me. Strange as it may sound, at that moment I think even the ascended masters and angels were struggling to contain themselves. They were giving off an air of so much excitement they were almost bursting out of their spiritual bodies.

Such was the brilliance of the Light emanating from the angel as it came to a halt in front of me I found myself having to lower my head a fraction. Only then did I see for the first time what the ascended masters and other angels already knew. The angel had a gift for me. What a truly wondrous gift it was. Wide awake, and cradled in the crook of the angel's arm, was a new-born child. It took all my powers of concentration just to breathe normally. Trying to embrace and absorb the golden energy and Light being projected from the child required every ounce of energy I possessed. Neither before nor since then have I seen reflective Light of such luminous gilded intensity. I do not know how I can put into words the moment the angel leant forward and placed the child into my outstretched arms. I was completely overcome with symphonies of profound emotions. Looking down on the sweet, gentle features of the child I recognised the existence of perfection. The extraordinary energy and Light of this golden child seemed to sear the centre of my entire being. I was completely seduced and entranced by the love in its heart and the purity of spirit deep within its newly found soul.

As I try to reflect on what happened next I would have to say that everything began to blur around the edges a little. Incapable of forming any real discernible thought, I was nonetheless conscious of every ascended master, archangel and angel as they closed ranks and came to stand around me and the child. How can I describe what that collective energy and experience felt like? Would well-versed superlatives such as extraordinary, incredible, astonishing, phenomenal, staggering or stupendous do justice to the whole experience, or was it simply out of this world and too mind-blowing for words? I opened my heart as wide as I could, and without uttering one syllable, asked the question I knew needed answering. Was this what it felt like when the hand of God reached down to touch someone in Blessing?

Reluctant to let go, I stayed in that space and place for the length of time that was gifted to me. One by one the ascended masters, archangels and angels appeared to turn and honour the child. Before walking away each reached out to touch the child in silent blessing. The child did not depart with them. I still had a short time to hold and gaze into the all seeing and knowing eyes of this miraculous golden blessing from God.

The child was gone and I was on my own once more. The pull on my emotions and senses was undeniably powerful and strangely contradictory. My previous joyful state and sense of living the Light was replaced with other, less positive sensations. I was left feeling bereft, saddened and abandoned, almost as though I had been cast adrift somehow. My heart was oddly weighted with the departure of all the celestial energies. I wanted the embrace of their energy and Light to enfold me once more.

With little or no idea of just how much time had elapsed, I found myself sitting alongside others in the circle and once again fully conscious of the workshop going on around me. There could be no denying the intensity of the energy in the room.

Many people had their own profound and unique experiences with celestial energies that afternoon. After my experience I did my best to reconnect and participate with the workshop group, but in all honesty it was really all a bit half-hearted. My mind could not detach itself from the encounter with the ascended masters and the golden child. All I wanted to do was to take time out and think about what had just happened. Why had I been singled out to receive such a unique and beautiful gift? What did it all mean?

Over the next few days I sought to discover the message behind the gift and the symbolism attached to it. What I was told was that the child represented a new golden age. In every country around the world very special children were being born. These children were exceptional in ways we did not even fully understand ourselves. Their intellect and ability to empathise and bring people together was simply staggering. On a spiritual level they were extraordinarily gifted. The powers they possessed would help us rediscover our commitment to life and encourage us to reconnect to the giver of that life. As a whole, the world would reawaken and discover the truth about Self and the one thing that gave meaning to their lives. That thing was the restoration of Faith and spiritual fulfilment. It was the only thing that would bring about harmony and a sense of oneness. More importantly than that was the knowledge that this fulfilment and sense of completeness would be responsible for the greatest gift to life. It would nurture the soul in a way nothing else could.

the road back to truth

Reflecting on the magnificent gift I had been given really made me take time out to think about the way I had lived my life up to that point. Should I have taken more care and placed greater attention and done things differently? I don't know the answer to that. As I reviewed the path I had chosen to walk several things rose up to meet me.

Deep down in my heart I always knew there was an unspoken understanding and expectation that change would have to take place. It had been a long time coming. Whether it was a conscious decision or not, somewhere in the grand scheme of evolving many people around the world had strayed from the true path and in the process had lost their way. An era of reckoning and acceptance of this fact was now upon those people. It was relatively easy to recognise myself as one of those wayward souls. Before a point of no return was reached all of us would be held accountable for being so cavalier in our attitude towards God. Why had we let so many of His precious gifts slip through our fingers? What was it that had led us to become so careless and selfish and obsessed with Self?

Anyone with a degree of sense could tell that a shift in consciousness had taken place. When the time came for people to reflect on this shift they would realise it wasn't necessarily a shift for the betterment of humanity. Self had become pre-eminent and as a result occupied many a mind. As people rushed headlong into the experience of living their lives in the fastest lane possible their focus shifted. Little room was left over for anything else. In standing by the choices they made, some of what people once held precious was abandoned along the way. A gradual and tangible air of inevitability managed to find a way of superimposing itself over some spiritual aspects of people and their lives. After that it was easy. In no time at all, many of God's children began turning their backs on Him. When they found themselves drifting away from Him why hadn't they tried harder to hold on? Perhaps people just found it easier and more convenient to their lifestyles not to think of Him at all. Maybe they mistakenly believed that they had strayed too far from Him and there was no road back. If a way did exist it was probably too arduous a journey to attempt. Sidelining God and putting him on back burner wasn't necessarily a deliberate act. I think people just became complacent in the knowledge that God could be pulled out of the hat, so to speak, whenever the need arose. He was the ace up the sleeve. Even if belief in God was wavering, He could always be counted upon to come to the rescue, couldn't He?

Who amongst those who once believed in God can say they fully understand the reasons for the slow and gradual demise of God in their lives, or the gradual abandonment of God from their lives? None of us should really be surprised that a new and more progressively enlightened generation now seeks to redress the balance and help raise the consciousness of the world once more. After our faltering commitment towards the Light, who are we to complain? We should be rejoicing that God holds steadfast in his love for us and has sent an extraordinary generation of enlightened ones to show us the way back onto the path of Truth.

As I continue to reflect, I don't think many people were necessarily shocked when they observed humanity beginning its steady fall into confusion and disarray. Comfortably ensconced in our own little bubbles of daily living, I do not imagine many of us gave more than passing consideration to consequences of our actions, or the knock-on effect they might have. It was not a case of maliciously or deliberately trying to undermine God; I think attention was focused elsewhere. As the world casually watched the gradual disintegration of God's greatest gift, one thing started to become abundantly clear. Even in a world where best intentions are voiced daily, none of us were innocent bystanders in humanity's slip from Grace. We freely and liberally gave ourselves permission to become participants in promoting changes to our lives and that of the universe which weren't always in the best interest of either. It was so easy for us to get caught up in the groundswell of non-resistance and self-congratulatory approval.

Instead of celebrating the joys of living in the world, we became back seat drivers and often let others steer a course for us. The road we were guided on was not always the good or right road for us as individuals or humanity in general, yet by avoiding ownership and abrogating responsibility we allowed certain events to formulate and unfold. We became lazy with the gift of life. So long as we were not inconvenienced or directly affected by events, we didn't feel the need to stand up and lay claim or take ownership of what followed. If we could live without our consciences pricking us too much, then we seemed perfectly content to sit back and quite literally watch the world go by.

There was a sense of predictability in the knowledge that a price would have to be paid for our carelessness and disregard. Although what I am about to say next can quite possibly be seen as a mass over generalisation, our preoccupation with our own lives left us insensitive to, and incapable of fully taking on, any sort of responsibility for what was happening all around us. Whether this was a calculated move on our behalf is, I suppose, open to debate. We certainly seemed blissfully unaware as negativity, corruption, greed and other hideous malevolent invaders slipped beneath our normally caring radar. Because we had become desensitised to certain aspects of our lives, we didn't really appreciate we were coming under attack. Suddenly, we found ourselves out of our depth and struggling to stay afloat. Faced with an insidious, negative malaise of gargantuan proportions, the precious world we once knew very quickly found itself edging towards crisis. The repercussions from this did not just stop at our own door. It stretched all around the world. When we finally woke up to the casual way we had empowered such negative forces, it didn't take long for us to realise the error of our ways. It was devastating to think that the responsibility for the ascendency of the ensuing darkness infiltrating the rhythm of the heartbeat of the world rested very firmly on our shoulders. It pervaded giant swathes of daily life with its potency. Somehow, we had to claw back what we had lost. As inhabitants of the planet, we as individuals would have to try to make amends and turn things around.

People quickly began to realise the days of materialism and self-gratification no longer succeeded in feeding the expanding void inside them. If the world had any chance of saving itself from the slippery, darkened pit it had fallen into then Truth, Faith and Love had to be recovered and placed at the forefront of our consciousness once more. Our style of living had to change and we as individuals had to change right along with it.

Tackling a task so enormous couldn't be something to be taken on singlehandedly. We were going to need help if Light was to be restored to the world. THAT was the message and the gift the golden child blessed me with that day.

I don't know if I was aware of it at the time, but work to restore the Light had already begun. What surprised me the most was being told that Children of the Light would stand by our sides and accompany us every step of the way. Blessed with very special gifts from God they would lead us out of the Darkness and into a place where Light embraced us once more.

As I look back on the day of the golden child and my divine encounter with ascended masters and angels all those years ago, I charge myself to remember each and every day just how precious and precarious the balance of life and living is, and how important it is to nurture the gift of life. If you believe nothing else I have put down on paper then believe this. NEVER forget that no matter how dark your life may seem at times as you travel your path, Light will ALWAYS prevail. By honouring that knowing, every day you surround yourself with Light in your life and love in your heart. If enough people believe in that then humanity will remember what it is like to live with the Light and in the Light. In the process of reawakening and rediscovering the God connection balance can and will be restored.

angelic connection

Seldom does a day of mine pass without angels playing some part in it. Communication might occur once a day, or perhaps several times a day. It greatly depends on what I am doing and who I have around me. The contact may last a minute or it may last an hour. I am so comfortable and used to having angelic energy around me it would seem really strange to have no access to or interaction with that energy.

One of the angels I work with more than most is one I christened the aqua angel. She came into my life over a decade ago. Ever since that day she has been a sounding board and a voice of calm optimism and reasoning. On the occasions I have felt utterly alone and abandoned she has been a listening ear and a source of great support and comfort. When the interminable hours of darkness march steadfastly forward, and isolation tightens it hold and I need help the most, she is always there for me. I don't know if it is common practice for people in general to have favourite angels or not, or if I should even be giving the impression that this particular angel should be called 'my' angel and therefore somehow exclusive to me, BUT when it comes to angels 'my' aqua angel really does hold a special place in my heart.

From our very first encounter I felt a strong pull towards her energy. Any type of angelic connection is an extraordinary event, but the connection I share with the aqua angel is unique and always seems to touch me at the deepest level. Although I know she is at any given time but a breath away, I do not always call upon her when seeking angelic assistance. Many times over the years I have called upon her and asked her to help me in assisting others. As a result, several of my friends experiencing some of the bleakest moments of deep personal crisis have been blessed by her presence. By appearing before them and wrapping her energy around them she was able to ease the pain and distress they had been experiencing. I know her energy was a tremendous comfort to two of my friends in the final stages of their lives. The gratitude I feel for such blessings really knows no bounds.

I am always astounded by the Light showered upon me by the aqua angel. It is quite unlike anything else I have experienced and therefore impossible to compare. My aqua angel is one of only a few celestial energies to have a strong defining feminine influence. There is an innate something about her ability to instantly calm and reassure. Every time I seek her help, she responds. Within a matter of seconds of calling out to her I am immersed in the most exquisite pale, crystalline, aqua coloured energy. Softly at first, it swiftly merges into a glistening, cascading force. It washes over every particle of my being, making me feel protected and loved and without fear. It is a truly amazing sensation to be part of that liquid embrace.

There has never been any real desire or need on my part to discover if my aqua angel has a name. For whatever reason, it is enough that I know her energy is near. I do remember at the very beginning when those first tentative connections were made wondering if the angelic energy I was experiencing was that of Lady Patience, the feminine counterpart to Sandalphon who is charged with anchoring Light on Earth. I have no recollection whatsoever if that brief moment of wondering was responded to in any way. It couldn't have been that pressing a matter for I pursued it no further. I have never given any further thought to it again until this very moment of writing the memory. Before I move on with additional writings, there is one final thing to share about the aqua angel. Even after all our years of connecting, my beautiful aqua angel is always capable of surprising me. Her energy can be so extraordinarily dynamic and powerful, yet at the same time, if required, she can be incredibly gentle and nurturing. I am so blessed to be able to connect with her energy.

Normally, when I work along with angelic energy I am conscious of a specific energy emanating from each and every one of those angels. It is a tangible source of inspiration and blessing. Arriving through a whispered veil of soft and delicate fragrance, each angel normally projects energy of exquisite colouring and varying dimension. If you ask most people who work with energies they will in all probability respond by describing angels coming to stand before them with feathered wings, glowing features and a heavenly presence. That is not the way it is for me. I don't know why only a very few angels ever respond to me by appearing in that particular form. I can immediately sense the presence of angels and see the magnificent colour surrounding them. I can even feel the extent of their energy, yet I very rarely see them as others might see them.

Every time angels respond to a call, the energy and Light they project is, in my experience anyway, something that is unique to that specific angel. The experience you share with your particular angel/s should always be regarded as something very special. It is something to marvel and cherish and take into your heart. Embrace this wonderful gift from the messenger God has chosen to send to you.

the advancement of angels into people's consciousness

People respond very differently whenever angels are mentioned. I am always intrigued by the reactions of others when talk of angelic and celestial energies arises. If you take the likes of me and my fellow believers in angels out of the equation, you are left with perhaps two or three other camps of thought. Before I start writing about these groups I have one small proviso. I think it is a point worth mentioning. Not everyone who decides to set out on a spiritual journey will necessarily encounter angels or what we might regard as celestial experiences. In other words, people can and do journey without angelic input, and in the process have extraordinary spiritual experiences. Each must seek their own path and what feels right for them.

In the first of the groups alluded to above, people generally show little or no inclination at all to explore anything which might be identified or regarded as being in the least bit spiritual. This particular group will forever sit on the fence when it comes to angels. Many of them might hold onto a tenuous acceptance of angelic existence, but for every one who thinks that way there are just as many who aren't quite so sure. Although they are confident enough in themselves and open to discussing angelic participation in others' lives, seldom do they end up truly believing in the possibility of angelic involvement in their own lives.

The next group of people are those who are genuinely interested in finding out as much as they can about angelic energies. They long to have their own experiences and encounters with celestial energies. I love working with and being around people in this category. It is an incredibly joyful and rewarding time for the recipients as they open themselves up to experience those first angelic connections. Watching someone set out on their spiritual journey is always such a privilege and joy.

Finally, we come to the last category in our group of three. There is an air of inevitability about the next words I lay down on paper. It would be almost impossible not to occasionally encounter individuals who very definitely do not believe in the existence of angels in any way shape or form. They may believe in a God, but the whole concept of angels is a complete anathema to them and leaves them feeling slightly incredulous of others' beliefs and definitive views. If I hadn't experienced this for myself I would not have believed how intensely people disagree on the topic of angelic energy. Emotions can and do run high. Admittedly, it is only a small minority who believe so passionately, but they can become extremely vociferous, almost to the point of belligerence about what they believe God's honest truth to be. I would even go as far as to say some people can be aggressive as they determine to take a stand against talk of angels. I have seen this happen so often. So keen are they to disprove others' theories and experiences, they possibly don't realise the impression they project. It is a great shame when people become so discomfited and agitated over another person's simple belief. In taking their stance they show great determination and spirit but the hostility which attaches itself to that stance is at times so palpable you can almost reach out and touch it. Displaying such frustration speaks volumes. Showing an inability to articulate and get their message successfully across to others can at times end up just confusing the issue.

Many non-believers have an expectation that believers in angels hear what they are saying, yet they themselves show little or no interest in opening themselves up to showing a respect and understanding of the belief system of others. I would not say all the time or even part of the time, but occasionally they are of the opinion that believers are rather sad, deluded individuals. In order to give meaning to our lives and make ourselves feel good we just make up our experiences with angels. This saddens me a great deal. Why such a negative reaction to other people's experiences? In a world where free choice and free will reign, there is room for whichever belief system any person chooses. The world is big enough to embrace all thought and beliefs.

On a personal note, I have never felt it is my job to try and explain myself and convince others of my connection or experiences with angels, or indeed any of the other energies I regularly work with. If people are curious and ask questions I am always more than happy to respond to their curiosity. I know the doubters out there far outweigh the believers, but things are definitely changing. The fact that angels are now openly talked about across all sectors must be seen as a plus and beneficial in raising awareness and spiritual consciousness. After that it is up to each individual to use the information in any way they may choose.

When I observe the rigidity and inflexible attitude many of those non-believers continue to hold onto I smile inwardly. It does make me curious at times if their belief is as absolute as they profess. I wonder if any of them ever listen to others talking about direct requests made to parking space angels or traffic light angels. Is such talk just automatically kicked into touch? Are the doubters or non-believers tempted in any way to give the idea room in their head, or are the angels summarily dismissed out of turn? Is the merest suggestion of angelic intervention such as this the litmus paper which ignites derision and ridicule, or is it a case of their curiosity being ignited?

I wonder briefly just how many people have felt the frustration of being at the mercy of the actions of others. Imagine if you will the scenario of being stuck in nose-to-tail traffic. When normally calm demeanour flies out the window and it becomes all too apparent that almost everyone in front is searching for that elusive parking space. As ever-vigilant traffic wardens patrol the pavements, people pray to see the lights of a car reversing. It becomes a battle of wills, with drivers refusing to move forward until the very last second. Just as the first foray into road rage tempts, a parking slot suddenly appears out of thin air. How did that happen you ask yourself? Recalling such events triggers other classic examples of serendipitous moments in time. What about those interminable queues at traffic lights? We have all experienced them at some time or other. With thoughts of beating the lights and getting through before they turn to amber the foot comes perilously close to pressing down on the accelerator again. As the car in front slows down and amber then red flashes you know you will not make it through. Not this time anyway. How does it make you feel when your silent pleading words to the angels are heard? When the red light inexplicably turns to green and the traffic gets under way again do you still have doubts about the existence of angels and your words having been heard?

Whichever path you decide to take and whatever viewpoint you hold on angelic energies, always try to have an open mind. I was almost fifty before I discovered the true blessing of angelic connection. A life without that daily communication and interaction with angels would sadden me in a way few other things could. Angels have opened my heart and helped me to live in Grace from a place of Truth and Love, and for that incredible gift I thank them from the bottom of my heart.